I0155232

Beauty's Way

Beauty's Way

Inspiration on the Path of Awakening

Lori Myles-Carullo

BALBOA.
PRESS
A DIVISION OF HAY HOUSE

Copyright © 2011 Lori Myles-Carullo.

All rights reserved. No part of this book may be used or reproduced by any means,
graphic, electronic, or mechanical, including photocopying, recording, taping or by any
information storage retrieval system without the written permission of the publisher
except in the case of brief quotations embodied in critical articles and reviews.

ISBN: 978-1-4525-3717-7 (sc)
ISBN: 978-1-4525-3719-1 (e)
ISBN: 978-1-4525-3718-4 (hc)
Library of Congress Control Number: 2011913024

Balboa Press books may be ordered through booksellers or by contacting:

Balboa Press
A Division of Hay House
1663 Liberty Drive
Bloomington, IN 47403
www.balboapress.com
1-(877) 407-4847

Because of the dynamic nature of the Internet, any web addresses or links contained in
this book may have changed since publication and may no longer be valid. The views
expressed in this work are solely those of the author and do not necessarily reflect the
views of the publisher, and the publisher hereby disclaims any responsibility for them.

The author of this book does not dispense medical advice or prescribe the use
of any technique as a form of treatment for physical, emotional, or medical
problems without the advice of a physician, either directly or indirectly. The
intent of the author is only to offer information of a general nature to help you
in your quest for emotional and spiritual well-being. In the event you use any
of the information in this book for yourself, which is your constitutional right,
the author and the publisher assume no responsibility for your actions.

Any people depicted in stock imagery provided by Thinkstock are models,
and such images are being used for illustrative purposes only.
Certain stock imagery © Thinkstock.

Printed in the United States of America

Balboa Press rev. date: 8/24/2011

"A beauty-full book, one that calls us back to source with its heart on its sleeve. With clarified language and imagery, Lori shares her journey with us, reminding us that we are not alone on our quest for magnificence. Lovely."

Jeff Brown, Author of *Soulshaping: A Journey of Self Creation* & *Apologies to the Divine Feminine*

"As flowers grow out of mud, Lori has cultivated a garden of beauty out of chaos, through learning to open her heart to love. In her remarkable story of self-discovery, we hear a vibrant voice of wisdom and compassion – a voice of hope for all who are searching to find a depth of meaning in the face of life's challenges."

Stephen Sims, Author of *River of Awareness* & Founding Director of IASIS (The Awareness Project)

"*Beauty's Way* is a gentle but powerful invitation to embrace the healing power of beauty that surrounds each of us. It is a potent reminder of the call to love. Thank you, Lori, for sharing your wisdom with the world. Indeed you have lived the path of 'healer'."

Barbara Burke, Author and Illustrator of *I Am Divine*, Supervising Teacher for Hoffman Institute Canada, & Principal of *Luminous Creations*

For Nicole:
my beloved friend whose beauty far surpasses
the illusory boundaries of life and what lies beyond.

And in honour of the beauty that shines
eternally and unconditionally within us all.

"Beauty is not in the face;
beauty is a light in the heart."
Kahlil Gibran

Contents

Preface: The Beginning before Beginning   1

The call to awaken *1*

Personal beauty journey *3*

Beauty source *8*

Part I: Honouring the Beauty of the East

Chapter 1 The Beauty of Awakening   17

Waking up to truth *17*

Awakenings *19*

The gift of waking up *21*

Awakening's call: a dream *24*

Beauty tips for awakening *25*

Chapter 2 The Beauty Of Joy   27

Defining joy *27*

Buddha-full joy *28*

Living joy *30*

Beauty tips for joy *34*

Chapter 3 The Beauty Of Change   35

Nature of change *35*

Change that heals *37*

Fashionable change *39*

Change + acceptance = inner peace *41*

Beauty tips for change *44*

Part II: Honouring the Beauty of the South

Chapter 4 The Beauty of Love   47

Fear of love *47*

Love is *49*

Big loves *51*

Beauty tips for love *64*

Chapter 5 The Beauty of Friendship   65

Heart-bonds *65*

Purifying fires *67*

Angel-friend *69*

Giving and receiving *72*

Beauty tips for friendship *74*

Chapter 6 The Beauty of Freedom   75

The attraction to freedom *75*

The dream of freedom *76*

Free to be *77*

I am free *78*

Freedom's divine structure *81*

Beauty tips for freedom *83*

Part III: Honouring the Beauty of the West

Chapter 7 The Beauty of Pain   87

The voice of pain *87*

Conscious pain *90*

Pain and suffering *90*

Pain's deeper mysteries *91*

Beauty tips for pain *95*

Chapter 8 The Beauty of Fear   97

Dissecting fear *97*

Fears big and small *101*

Through fear to love *102*

Beauty tips for fear *107*

Chapter 9 The Beauty of Gratitude   109

Gratitudinal vibrations *109*

No complaints *110*

The light of gratitude *111*

Beauty tips for gratitude. *115*

Part IV: Honouring the Beauty of the North

Chapter 10 The Beauty of Grief   119
Grief roots. *119*
Surrendering to grief: feeling the feelings *121*
Love and loss. *123*
Big, conscious, magic grief *127*
One more time *131*
Beauty tips for grief. *133*

Chapter 11 The Beauty Of Forgiveness   135
Giving forth love. *135*
Binding in guilt, releasing in innocence *138*
Forgiveness school *139*
I'm sorry. *142*
The miracle. *143*
Beauty tips for forgiveness. *146*

Chapter 12 The Beauty of Peace   149
Degrees of inner peace *149*
Peace-busters. *151*
My piece of peace. *155*
Beauty tips for peace *163*

Afterword: A New Beginning   165
Divine completion. *165*
Love letter. *166*

Acknowledgments   169

Preface:

The Beginning before Beginning

The call to awaken

There is a sacred and delicious way of living life on this crazy, beautiful planet, a way of life that is full of joy, expansive in love, and characterized by deep peace. We have the sweet capacity to awaken into this extraordinary manner of living any moment we consciously choose to. Many of us don't realize that the choice exists, yet even if we do, we often feel powerless to tap into it. Many people of all races, religions, and creeds have been honourably walking, living, breathing, and dancing in search of balance and harmony for thousands if not millions of years. It is Beauty's Way, the path that is guided by the awakening heart and characterized by bringing love to all aspects of life: to the light, to the dark, and to every subtle shade in between. This beautiful path has been inspiring me for many years to share her universal message. Beauty's Way is open and accessible to all, with no exceptions.

All that I share in this book is in service to exploring and celebrating Beauty's Way as it has presented itself consistently in my life experiences. A treatise on this way of life and love has been yearning to be written through me for many years, and it has patiently yet persistently awaited its time of fruition. Its call has ranged from soft, almost inaudible whispers to loud and potent screams that awaken me in the night, unyielding in urgency. I have been deeply blessed to have the uncommon luxury of time and space within which to actually materialize the thoughts and inspirations flowing through me, and I am filled with gratitude and humility at the prospect of finally making this longstanding dream a lived reality. The inner call to create has become impossible to deny or repress.

It seems to me that the bells of awakening are tolling louder and more frequently these days, and I say that not just because we are nearing the epic year 2012. The ancient Mayan calendar is nearing completion of a major cycle, and many among us wonder if this might signify a grand shift in our planet and the collective consciousness. My lived experience of the wave of awakening ebbing and flowing and gaining greater strength and power comes from witnessing my own rhythmical inner process of transformation and bearing witness to the people I am surrounded by, both as friends and clients, doing their healing work. What I see is an increasing number of brave souls waking up to truth and shedding the various veils of illusion that threaten to blind them to the beauty inherent in this life when it is radically embraced with love.

We, as brothers and sisters in the family of humanity, are implored by the Spirit of Life herself to walk alongside one another on this wild and wonderful journey. We are urged to grow and evolve psychologically and spiritually in order to become truly liberated from our past conditioning and destructive mental and emotional patterns. I was recently exposed to some interesting statistics concluding that the critical mass needed to make a major shift in consciousness for the whole human race is only 4.7 percent of the population. My first instinctual response to that information was one of shock: "Really? Is that it? And we're not there yet?!" I guess we're not. Yet I can't help but be optimistic about the miraculous ripple effects that will come from all the sacred growth work being done on both individual and collective levels as the beauty of peace and love expands across the globe.

Personal beauty journey

What does beauty have to do with all of this? My most simple and honest response is: everything. A more complete answer will unfold as I share my thoughts, reflections, anecdotes, and inspirations through the various chapters of this book, drawing from my own rich and diverse life experiences and offered generously by others on the beauty path. My healing journey through the course of this lifetime has been full of much love and also many challenges. In times of intense pain and struggle, I felt like I was going to hell and back so many times that I was building up frequent flyer miles to VIP status. Unfortunately, I am not exaggerating.

There were many times when literally all I could do was breathe in and breathe out; each repetition of that sequence was, in and of itself, a small yet mighty victory. Living in this particular body as such a sensitive being sometimes seemed wrong. I felt that if I were truly meant to be here on this earth, I would have been equipped in ways that would make this experience somewhat easier, especially considering I believe in a loving and kind God who is mysteriously and miraculously interested in the well-being of each and every one of his creations. Even when my life felt unbearably fragile and circumstances were tougher than tough, in my heart I felt a divine force of love and light awakening, urging me to never give up. I was being called to continue planting conscious seeds of hope and faith in life's ultimate goodness. For whatever reason or purpose, I was to make something exquisitely beautiful from the depths of my pain instead of allowing it to embitter and drown me in despair.

I have always been quite spiritual in my outlook on life and have consistently longed to find a sense of deeper meaning. A highly energetic child, my sensitive gastrointestinal system got the best of me in my early teens when I became ill with parasites on a family trip to Western Canada. The parasitic infection went undiagnosed for three years, at which point I developed Chronic Fatigue Syndrome (CFS). Sadly, not a single doctor thought to check for parasites despite extensive testing by highly respected professionals in the

Western, allopathic tradition. After those three years of internal struggle and fighting, my immune system was so run-down that I was left weak and vulnerable. I felt like I was closer to ninety years old than sixteen.

Thus my first wake-up call in life came through a personal health crisis. CFS stopped me dead in my tracks, and my train used to run at warp speed. I could no longer eat whatever I wanted as I developed many food and environmental sensitivities, I couldn't go to school on a regular basis, and the dance classes I loved were now out of the question. The list went on and on in terms of what was taken away from me during those years. It didn't seem fair, and I wondered what might be wrong with me. What kind of karma was I living out to find myself in such a compromised position when all my friends and family seemed so healthy and "normal"? There I was, completely at the mercy of this strange disease named by three dreaded letters. It is now more explicitly defined as ME, a virus related to polio called Myalgic Encephalomyelitis, a medical term that basically means that the disease affects the muscles and the brain. All I knew was that, whatever the label, I had no way of knowing if or when I would ever feel good again.

As I recall those years of illness, there are experiences and feelings that I remember and many things I believe my compassionate psyche lovingly helped me to forget. I have an inkling that this experience is similar to women giving birth and forgetting how agonizing the process was so that they might consider procreating again. Maybe. But the best way I can describe my experience is to say that it was similar to being struck by a nasty flu bug. I felt chronically weak, dizzy, tired, and nauseous; my eyes burned, my head ached, and my whole sense of balance and well-being felt "off." All I wanted to do was lie down and stay down. But unlike the flu, it didn't just last a few days; with little variation, I felt that way for more than two and a half years. This strange virus took over my whole body and being, and ripped me apart from my friends and the full life I used to enjoy.

Looking back, I feel deeply thankful that my spirit remained hopeful and kept reaching out to a force greater than myself, a power I lovingly refer to as God, for comfort, strength, and moments of relief. Often the mystical within us awakens when we suffer deeply and are thus inspired to transcend the heaviness of our human experience for survival's sake. Before I was granted the diagnosis of CFS, I feared that I had cancer or AIDS and the doctors just hadn't found it yet. The predominant feeling was one of something being very, very wrong inside me, and I didn't know how it would ever be made "right" again. Being sick taught me a great deal about what it means to heal, because I needed to put all my life energy into becoming well if I wanted to ever feel good and participate in the flow of the greater world again.

I learned about the systems of the body, the life of the cells, the importance of what we think and feel, and how those thoughts and feelings affect our well-being. I listened to relaxing music with healing subliminal messages, and was guided in my first visualization meditation. I can still envision myself diving down a huge waterfall into a calm pond thick in the embrace of nature. In my mind's eye, I relaxed and bathed in the pure, restorative water while the purely loving presence of Jesus held me in his arms and offered me his light, healing, and unconditional love. I started eating healthy foods, took more supplements than I had ever seen in my life, and received B12 shots regularly in the butt in an effort to jump-start myself with some energy. I tried to talk to friends about what I was going through and did my best to live a regular teenage life. And yet, when I pushed myself to do this, I simply collapsed and needed time to recover. I lovingly vowed not to over-exert myself like that again. That is, until the next time. I did the same thing all over again simply because I wanted *to live!*

In the midst of this dark time, I knew very well that I could either slump into deep depression (which I did sometimes) or I could do my best to be compassionate with myself, right where I was, and put my energy into finding the beauty within each day's gifts. When I allowed myself to connect, in gratitude, with all that was still beautiful and good, I breathed a little easier and found sparks of joy in small blessings that otherwise I would have unconsciously overlooked. I would catch the exquisite color explosion of the setting sun, streaming warm golden light with flashes of turquoise and brilliant fuchsia through my bedroom window, and I would remember the divine artistry of a loving God, painting the sky simply for our delight. I would answer the phone call of my best friend, Penny, and we would read together the daily inspiration from a book entitled *Silent Strength*. I felt the tender gift of loving friendship from this angel girl who was, and still is, there for me through thick and thin.

I would wait eagerly each day for my father to come home from work, who sought me out simply to hold my hand and listen to how I was feeling. From the purest intentions of fatherly love, he was present to me in the best way he knew how, and that carried a beauty of its own. I can't imagine how tough that must have been for him to see me, his youngest daughter, flat on her back and struggling on a daily basis when he knew how much life, energy, and potential I had within me. I sensed that he saw me—the *real me* beyond the *sick me*—and that in itself was a gift. I gave thanks for the sweet and simple offering of spring tulips or sunflowers placed in my room by my mother, a token of her caring and wish for me to be blessed by some life and beauty even if most things seemed lifeless and bleak.

Beauty, revealed in a multitude of love-expressions, was always present if I was willing to behold it and give thanks. And there was always someone I could connect to and bless, even if it meant offering a prayer, sending a note, or giving a call simply to let people know that they were loved. Even if the parasites and virus had gotten the better of me for a while, eating away at me on the inside and recklessly stealing my vital life force, I was determined that I would not be a parasite only receiving nourishment without giving any back.

These are just a few of the many facets of my healing journey, which took many years and much hard work. I had a wonderful medical doctor in Toronto who also worked holistically, and he taught me much about what it means to nourish the body and boost immunity. My counsellor gave me space to explore my emotions and belief systems, and to feel supported psychologically and spiritually. I had a few good friends who didn't give up on me just because my life had changed dramatically. And my family did their best to lovingly witness my process, step by step. I feel incredibly fortunate to have overcome CFS and to be living now at a much higher level of wellness than ever before.

The first time I recovered from the illness was two and a half years after my first diagnosis. I literally woke up one day, having fulfilled my body's need to get to a warm climate during a chilly Canadian winter, and felt almost symptom-free. It was a strange sensation for me at first, because it had been so long since I had been well. And yet, the feeling remained and I was able to get back into a full life. Being healthy again felt ecstatic, and I never took a moment of well-being for granted. Unfortunately I had a relapse of the illness in my mid-twenties (six years after my first recovery), sparked by a new infection that once again weakened my immune system. The symptoms of the sickness for the next few years were much less intense than in the first occurrence, however CFS once more had a hold on me that made my life more challenging.

It wasn't until I was in my thirties that I could truly say I had mostly recovered from the illness. It was a constant companion to me in my healing journey for a big part of my life, one that taught me a great deal about how vital it is that we be true to ourselves, and never give into giving up. In the final days of struggling with this illness, I chose to give new words to the letters CFS in order to affirm my ability to heal, giving neuro-linguistic programming a chance to work its magic. Yes, I had CFS: Courage, Faith, and Strength. Grateful to be well again, my passion for life and sense of greater purpose were reawakened with a new fire. The old tape of "I can't" was replaced with "I can" because of what I now believed to be possible.

I am awake to much more beauty now, perhaps because that experience of suffering carved out a deep space inside me to be open to life in a powerful way. Through the years, I have to come to understand the essence of beauty to be love. Love is the author of all miracles, and miracles are always possible. So, in the most basic and fundamental of terms, Beauty's Way is the way of love, and love is the sacred elixir in the bittersweet alchemy of life. We, as a human family on this planet, are in every moment capable and called upon to add more beauty and love to the world. It is vital that we support one another in acknowledging and letting go of our fears, and in sharing our struggles, hopes, and dreams. We have the amazing capacity to choose—one thought, word, and deed at a time—to love instead of hate, to create peace rather than war, to replace judgment with compassion, to sow seeds of hope rather than drown in despair. We can be creators, artists, servants, stewards, and heart-and-soul participants in a more beautiful world. We can, and for the sake of life itself, we must.

Beauty source

The term, "The Beauty Way," is born of the Navajo tradition. I was first introduced to this way of life while taking a course at the University of Toronto focused on Native American religions. Immediately, the very idea of the Beauty Way ignited a spark in me that sent shivers to my core, together with a deep inner knowing of something that was to be revolutionary in my life. In an article entitled *'Diné Bo'óhoo'aah Bindii'a': Navajo Philosophy of Learning'* in Volume 1 of the 1987 *Dine Bi'iina Journal*, Herbert J. Benally sums it up beautifully:

> When we recognize and activate the Divine Power-Within, we experience the Beauty Way of Life, *Hozhq*. Through this realization, we live with respect and reverence for all of creation. It is up to each one of us to inspire our youth to cherish and perpetuate beauty, peace, and joy as a Way of life.

In the process of feeling called to write this book and to share with the world an invitation to collectively walk in beauty, I have wondered if I might best present this information by first spending some time with the Navajo community, perhaps doing field research in New Mexico or Arizona or wherever the opportunity arose. I wanted to make sure that even though I am in no way an expert on the Navajo Beauty Way, I am honouring the Navajo people and their Way with utmost integrity. So I was thrilled in every cell of my being to receive an e-mail from the Institute of Traditional Medicine stating that they were privileged to be bringing to Toronto a medicine woman, Walking Thunder, from the Navajo tradition. It was to be her first time travelling outside the United States to share her wisdom and healing power. The timing of her arrival to my hometown was perfect for me. What a gift! Synchronicity can be very sweet.

In a flurry of enthusiasm, excitement, and overwhelming passion, I immediately e-mailed the director of the Institute and basically said: "Sign me up for everything Walking Thunder is offering!" This included two nights of lectures and healing ceremonies, an afternoon in which she was to demonstrate her sand-painting meditations, and a personal healing session with Walking Thunder herself. I booked one of the first private appointments available, and in the days leading up to meeting this revered medicine woman, I conjured up elaborate ideas for how this personal connection to the Navajo tribe and my time with Walking Thunder might inspire my life, including the writing of this book. I even had a fantasy of being invited to live with her and her family on her reservation in order to have a pure, authentic experience of walking in beauty!

In the end, she did inspire me greatly, and I am forever thankful. However, as often happens on life's path, this encounter did not turn out at all as I had planned, and yet it was perfect and divine.

I met with Walking Thunder on a Friday afternoon at 3:00 p.m. She took me into the consulting room where the healing magic was to take place. As we sat facing one another, she looked me deep in the eyes and with a great sense of calm and curiosity began asking me who I was and why I had requested a session with her. I told her that I was writing this book inspired by "The Beauty Way" of her tradition, and that I had been in the healing arts for many years. I expressed my strong desire to experience her knowledge, insights, inspiration, and healing. I truly believed that I was in for some sort of powerful shamanic session, that she would use her feathers, crystals, rattles, and whistles, and that she would smudge me with sage or sweetgrass and I would come out of that hour a new woman. I imagined that whatever happened in the healing presence of Walking Thunder would change my life forever.

Much to my surprise and absolute confusion, she refused to work with me. *What?!?* She said that the effort I was making with my healing work was all that was required. I just needed to believe more in myself and all that I was currently taking part in. She said that "The Beauty Way" had everything to do with how I was already living my life, and the essence of it was simply being who I am. She said, "You are good. You are strong. You are beautiful." In essence, Walking Thunder told me that there was nothing wrong with me and that it was against her tradition to do a healing for someone who didn't need it. And that was it. At about 3:10 p.m., I was walking out the door, having received all the medicine I required—an affirmation of my wellness and beauty and perfection just as I was. Beautiful. I attended her lecture and healing ceremony that night, and it was a delight to hear her tell stories and share laughter and witty wisdom with us all. At the end of the evening, I was left with even more of a sense that the Beauty Way is a universal call for all people to live from love in their awakening hearts and thus to create a more beautiful world. Walking Thunder's greatest message was: *Be who you are.*

Too often we forget who we really are as we get swallowed up both externally and internally by circumstances and our reactions to them. Thus, we suffer. The eyes of our heart, the doors of our mind, and the windows of our soul have been closed, and we sleepwalk through life rather than allow ourselves to live the thriving path of awakening. We think we are limited by and enclosed within our separate bodies, and we fall into the trap of believing that we have no control over our lives. In our mass delusion, we act as though what we think and feel has no real impact on ourselves or others. We are either blatantly or subtly ignorant of our true power and birthright as children of a loving God.

We become blind to the beauty of life that is right in front of our eyes longing for us to take a taste of its sweetness, to breathe in its fragrance, to simply cherish its all-encompassing existence. It is as if most or all of us are walking around blindfolded, perfectly capable of removing that which covers our eyes and limits our sight, yet choosing to fumble awkwardly in the dark because it has become our familiar, comfortable-although-uncomfortable safety zone. Better to settle for such a meagre existence than to step into the vast unknown, into the light, and not know what might come of such brightness! God forbid, it could be death! Or life ... We tend to be equally afraid of both in such a fear-full, paralyzed state.

Beauty's Way, in my personal understanding of it and my attempt to practice it daily, encourages us to live from the core of our tender hearts—raw, real, and vulnerable in the power and strength of the truth that shines within us, eternally and unabashedly. It is the Way beyond fear yet fully accepting of it, the Way beyond pain yet with great compassion for it, and the Way beyond doubt simply because faith brings so much more peace to our powerful yet fragile existence. Often, we humans only open to the truth that is love and come to accept this amazing grace that restores our true vision when things get so bad that *any* other way seems like it would be better than *this*, because *this* is not working, no matter how hard we try.

We have the sacred opportunity to become humbled quickly when in crisis. Life wakes us up when we are in the grips of heartache from yet one more shattered relationship, when there is a death in the family or the passing of a close friend, when we are diagnosed with a serious illness, or when we are plagued with a feeling of meaninglessness so dark and empty it feels hopelessly impenetrable. Despair and hurt can take on a thousand faces, yet at the root of the multitude of ways in which we suffer lies this deep desire for a taste of true freedom, for a new way of living that allows grace to shine through the thick, dark fog of a life lived in fear. Beauty's Way reminds us of the incredible gifts to be found in all aspects of life lived with an open, loving, and awakening heart.

Since this book is inspired by the Navajo tradition, I felt compelled to structure it according to the order, balance, and harmony of the medicine wheel, honouring the various dynamics of the cardinal directions, the elements of creation, and how our relationship to these is vital to the healing of the whole. Within each aspect of the wheel are different aspects of life in which we can always find, create, and participate in beauty. It doesn't matter if you are an ultra-chic, modern, urban dweller or a nature lover who is more familiar with the various aspects and energies of creation—we are all, each one of us, children of heaven and earth and everything in between. Harmony for one leads to harmony for all.

We are one big, multi-faceted human family, and it is up to us to create the life that we want for ourselves and for future generations. It is an interesting, challenging, and amazing time to be alive on this planet—a time when ancient spiritual and metaphysical truths are consistently being validated by quantum physics and other modern sciences, thereby acknowledging the principle of interconnectedness of all living things. As global residents and neighbours, we have had to bear the effects of conflicts and war, bizarre epidemics, a troubled economy, and natural disasters. In the face of such chaos and confusion, we have the chance to harness the power of our thoughts and heart-felt intentions help to create a new reality based on love and unity rather than fear and separation.

My greatest and most genuine prayer is that this book will bless you on your sacred life-path in a way that reawakens the natural beauty that forever lives within your heart, mind, body, and soul. I pray that the power of that awakened beauty radiates out in every direction to bless all that you encounter on this earth. Together, we are the precious ones called as love-filled warriors to ride the wave of this awakening force and to live from our heart wisdom in order to create a more beautiful, peaceful, love-filled world. We are the light-shiners, called not only to focus on increasing the light itself, but also to radiate our heart-light toward all that lies in the shadows. I invite you to join me on this holy journey. I am honoured to join with you.

In the name of love and beauty,
Lori Myles-Carullo

N.B. Throughout this book, I consciously chose to alternate using masculine and feminine pronouns in reference to God and other symbolic names for the Higher Power. I feel that the Divine encompasses the qualities of both genders, and also lies beyond such grammatical and/or linguistic delineations.

Part I:

Honouring the Beauty of the East

———

We turn our awakening hearts to the East and we give great thanks for:
The sweet gift of limitless new beginnings
Fresh, blank pages waiting with bated breath for poetic nourishment
White, empty canvases yearning for the textured touch of wet colours
Creativity exuberantly growing and thriving
The brilliant miracle of each perfect sunrise
Spring's soft, moist ecstasy
Hope for highly anticipated rebirth
Innocence and purity
The radiant, exuberant joy of a child who, in the moment, knows of nothing else
Courage to shine a single ray of light
Our gracious capacity to inhale and exhale through pain
Life's mysterious gift of a love that conquers all
HO!

Note: 'Ho!' is the syllable sounded in Native American traditions in order to join voices and energies together in affirming the truth, power, and beauty of what has just been offered.

Chapter 1

The Beauty of Awakening

"And the day came when the risk of remaining tight in a bud became more painful than the risk it took to blossom."
Anais Nin

"God has never been missed.
Maybe you have forgotten, that's all.
Maybe you have fallen asleep, that's all."
Osho

"May our heart's garden of awakening
bloom with hundreds of flowers."
Thich Nhat Hanh

Waking up to truth

Before exploring the many exquisite facets of our awakening, we must first acknowledge where we have been chronically fast asleep—and I don't mean the kind of sleep we all need in order to regenerate and recharge on a nightly basis. We have become dull sleepwalkers in our collective and personal ignorance of certain key truths, without which we are destined to remain in a state of sadness, loss, despair, craving, and on the whole, suffering. Such a state is gray, cold, lifeless, heavy, and energetically dense. Awakening is all about returning to our natural state of love and joy and following a path that forever puts us back on the perennial course of love when we detour into fear's dead-ends.

While walking early one morning along a mountainous road in north central Costa Rica, I was surrounded by lush green hills and cows pondering the abundance of a new day's grass. A light, refreshing rain began washing over me. By the side of the road, were many weeds and dusty plants, thirsting for wetness to soak in and nourish them in their low-to-the-ground lives. In the midst of the weeds, I found, to my delight, a beautiful little pink wildflower, brimming with the simple ecstasy of existence. She was so small that I had to kneel down in order to get a better look at her, and I was awed by how such a tiny part of existence could be so intricate in beauty. I observed the various shades and hues of pink at her bubble-like core, a hundred fragile tendrils making their way up to bright yellow nodules at the tip of each one. This little flower was clearly an exquisite gift of life, beautiful simply for beauty's sake, growing from the weeds and what seemed to be insignificant plant life on the side of the road. What a perfect metaphor for awakening.

This gorgeous little sparkle of life speaks brilliantly to how each of us has the capacity to transform through the grimy muck of our human lives, extracting exactly what is needed from the dust and ashes in order to arrive at our vibrant blossoming beyond the surface. Each of us is called by name to become the unique and precious flower of creation that radiates our true essence. If we are open enough to see things as they truly are, we find that we are often longing for that which we already possess. The Buddha found nirvana in his own way—under the bodhi tree, after years of extreme seeking for some sort of inner peace and freedom in the midst of the pain of human existence. He was gracious enough to dedicate the rest of his time on this earth to teaching the awakened practice of liberation in mind, body, and spirit from the suffering that inevitably comes from mental and emotional patterns based in fear and ignorance. Jesus, too, knew the truth of love that would set us free; and it was to this end that he taught, healed, prayed, and lived his life in a way that would forever remind humanity that life and love are far more powerful than death and fear. Amma, a modern saint of a woman, is hugging people into awakening on a daily basis. She is an inspiration to us all, proving that the loving power of the heart is truly what is needed in order to offset the tragic direction in which our world has been heading, blinded and paralyzed by fear.

Awakening is a pervasive, archetypal leitmotif that runs through a variety of spiritual and psychological traditions. There is an undeniable, collective yearning for a peace and happiness that transcends what we know and experience in the messy drama of everyday life. For the most part, we seek to escape the pain of our realities through addictions and obsessions that lead us farther away from our ultimate goal of peace. What originally promises to offer us everything we could ever want or need in order to save us from pain, ends up causing even more suffering and does nothing to heal the original wound. Ah, the bittersweet symphony of life here on earth. At the end of the day, many of us are often left with a lingering sense of emptiness and futility. As things go from bad to worse, we often give voice to the slightest glimmer of a hopeful thought:

"There *must* be another way."
"There is," Life whispers.
"There *must* be a better way."
"There is," Life sings.

And finally, we are brought humbly to our knees, and we stay there long enough to genuinely pray to a Higher Power, a Greater Force, a Spirit that hears and answers us as we find that we are willing to do whatever it takes to change our lives:

"God, please show me the way."
And she will …

Awakenings

Certain films come to mind as I consider the pop-culture images of awakening, each with its own impact. The first film is *Thelma*

& Louise, in which two women find themselves together on the run, rebelling against all that has caused them pain and suffering, fighting for their lives in both subtle and not-so-subtle ways. And men—please stay with me here—I know there can be a tendency for the male population to cross themselves and run the other way when they hear those two names; but the lesson is the same for us all, regardless of gender. The deep wounds of these two women—one stemming from a haunting past rape, and the other from a recent abusive relationship—lead them to go to extremes in order to taste freedom. It is, however, a radical and short-lived liberation, as their wild spirits lead them to courageously choose death over certain imprisonment.

The one scene from this movie that stands out starkly in my memory involves Thelma and Louise on the run, driving in their sleek convertible across the hot desert roads of the southern states. With little sleep and a high level of alcohol coursing through her veins, Thelma exclaims triumphantly, "I'm awake, Louise! I don't remember when I've ever been so awake." She is free from the chains of her abusive husband, and she is traveling an uncharted course that fills her with the ecstatic drunkenness of possibility. She is free from the old version of herself that kept her stuck in a torturous life she despised, yet endured, for the majority of her adult life. She is free to explore her sexuality in a new way that leaves her smiling from ear to ear with the knowingness of a woman in touch with her deepest hungers and longings. Despite the tragedy of how things end up for these two women, Thelma claims her moment of absolute freedom; and this is her personal, exuberant tale of radical awakening. Even if for just that moment, she knows that she deserves far more than what she had been accepting from life; that is enough to convince her that there is no going back.

A second gem of a movie that tells the story of a woman's journey of awakening is *Sirens,* starring Hugh Grant and Elle MacPherson. Grant plays a youthful Anglican priest traveling with his wife, Estelle, deep in the Australian outback. His theologically authorized mission is to attempt to redeem a local artist whose erotically charged and politically controversial paintings are deemed both vile and heretical by the Anglican Church. The young couple encounters their own sexual desires and demons as they are faced with the artist's radical views and lifestyle. Estelle is reluctantly yet alluringly befriended by the beautiful women who model for the artist. She curiously finds herself longing to be one of them rather than standing in cold judgment from the outside.

Estelle also experiences a surprisingly passionate attraction to the supposedly blind stable hand, which leads to a welling up of her natural feminine desires and challenges her rigid, externally imposed code of sexual morality. At the conclusion of the movie, there is an exquisite, sensual scene in which Estelle lies vulnerably still in a secluded pond, surrounded by the nymph-like women who are gently and tenderly caressing her naked body. It is a dreamy, mystical awakening that ushers in her rebirth—a seductive baptism into more of who she really is. The only sound that is heard above the rhythmic rush of water is her deep, soulful cry: "I want to wake up now." She is awake.

The gift of waking up

I feel like I've been dancing the dance of awakening for a long time, and this dance contains many steps, many rhythms, many variations. My awakening process is far from over, and I give thanks because it is such a fascinating journey. Many years ago when I lived nestled in the mountains of Whistler, British Columbia, I experienced many random, spontaneous moments of feeling as if I had been granted a precious treasure that I couldn't explain in words. This feeling seemed more real than anything I had ever experienced—a visceral, highly conscious sense of the truth beyond all illusions. The bliss of those tiny yet hugely satisfying tastes of awakening made it tough to come back to a regular life of working, serving customers, and balancing out the cash flow at the beginning and end of my retail shifts. At times I found it challenging to integrate the two worlds— the secular and the divine—and yet there was no way I could deny either one its reality in my day-to-day existence. I had my moments of ecstasy and epiphany and my daily routine of work and play, all merging in unique combinations and flowing into one interesting and amazing way of being.

When I moved to Western Canada for the first time at age twenty-one, I was experiencing a great deal of pain and sorrow due to the recent divorce of my parents and the resulting sting of emotional fallout. The precious spiritual times of deep letting go of all that was bringing me down—anger, resentment, sorrow, loss, and heartache——opened up space in my core for the pure, limitless sense of the loving power of creation to step up and take control again. My inner sense of the deep, loving interconnectedness of all living things was the most beautiful gift I could have received from the universe to remind me that the face of God was still a happy one.

Unlike many ski and snowboard enthusiasts living in Whistler at the time, I was not under the influence of any psychotropic substances (unless you count truly loving life as a drug!). Drops of awakening would graciously fall upon me and my unsuspecting consciousness without any warning or pattern. I received precious moments of awakening with gratitude and dwelled in them with a sense of delighted curiosity. Naturally, I always looked forward to when the next sweet drop of bliss might fall and land in every cell of my receptive being. Maybe I was getting "second-hand high" from all the marijuana being smoked around me, but I think it was God's grace at work. I was "first-hand high" in a natural and unadulterated way.

And what did I do with this sense of awakening to the truth of existence as love itself? I certainly couldn't keep it to myself or it would have been a crying shame. I also am not the type to preach at full voice on street corners or try to lure people into an experience that is deeply personal, divinely intimate, and lusciously mysterious to me. So, I just breathed, walked, ate, skied, slept, danced, worked, and smiled. I took that deep peace and solid inner confidence with me through my days and nights, and simply shined. At that time, I had the luck and the pleasure of working in one of the most popular and trendy nightclubs in Whistler village, which had just reopened after extensive renovations. I walked into work every night and radiated this awakened love to the staff members and any and all patrons I came across.

It was no secret that I was a bit of an anomaly to the other cocktail waitresses and bartenders. I hardly drank so I didn't do as well as the others most nights in terms of tips because I wouldn't get drunk with the customers. (What? A 'shooter' girl who doesn't do shots with her paying customers?! Is this possible?) Yet I was told time and time again by friends and strangers that my light was a curious and welcome blessing in that place. And why not? As Marianne Williamson stated in *A Return to Love*, we bring ourselves as ministers of God to wherever we are and however we are of service. So at that time, the bar was my church. The community changed every night, but my heart and soul remained consistently luminous and ready to share. We all contain the same divine spark; by sharing the beauty of love and light, each in our own unique ways, we are adding to the flame of awakening that burns bright all over the world.

We must practice living awakened lives, expressing ourselves and finding the energy fuelling us from within to truly live before life passes us by and we realize that we allowed fear to keep us stuck in our unconscious, ignorant, and limited dream-state. More and more people these days are seeking mentors and life coaches, attending seminars and workshops, and reading self-help books and listening to inspirational tapes and CDs to try to uncover passion and purpose in life and to gain the support and encouragement to actually live it. This is good and beautiful because, if we don't, what are we doing on this planet other than exchanging oxygen and carbon dioxide until our last breath? What are we doing for ourselves and for future generations if we don't wake up to the truth that love is the only thing that is truly real in this life, and that it is high time we stop putting so much energy into fear? Why wait until you are on your deathbed to realize that what really mattered most in this life was the love given and received? We are wasting precious time and energy in which we could be savouring the sweetness of life rather than complaining about its bitterness.

Awakening's call: a dream

Many years ago, life woke me up from my living dream of intense pain through a night dream that inspired great hope. At the time, I was struggling with a highly sensitive body due to the years of parasites and CFS, and I had developed an eating disorder that was based in fear and control. I was in pretty rough shape and in dire need of some divine intervention to save me from myself. Deeply afraid of life and becoming smaller and smaller in body and consciousness, I sensed awakening as something a long way away. Some part of me knew that the pain I was in and the unrelenting feeling of being imprisoned, locked away from health and vitality, were not going to hold me back forever. The very powerful dream I was graced with awakened me into my next steps toward healing. I was struggling with my dietary issues, unable to digest much of anything and afraid that everything would hurt me. The list of items that were "safe" for me to eat had gotten smaller and smaller with each passing day. I was five foot six inches and had just plummeted below one hundred pounds. My ribs ached in the morning from rubbing up against the bed beneath me. That was not the dream part; that was my nightmarish reality.

Then came awakening's call: my dream. I was in a taxi with an older man and I couldn't breathe, so I asked him to take me to the hospital. Instead, he took me to a church. I was perplexed, but I trusted him. He carried me into the sacred building on his shoulders. A goddess-like female minister was standing at the front of the church by the altar, and as the man began walking down the aisle between the pews, she held up her hand as if to say with a stern yet loving command, "Stop right there." She began to speak to us, and I remember listening very closely both to her wise words and to the tender tone of her angelic voice. Her first request was intended for him, and it included an admonition to put me down so that I could stand on my own two feet.

Once I was standing on solid ground, it was my turn. She gave me three distinct messages of guidance. She looked deeply into my eyes and directly into my soul and said, "First, you need to breathe. Next, you need to eat. And finally, you need to commune." That was it. I awoke with a sense of clarity and hope that before seemed lost. Very soon after that, I got a job at an oxygen bar serving medical-grade oxygen to health-striving customers and receiving more oxygen into my lungs and cells by taking my daily "hit." I slowly began to eat more nourishing foods and found myself able to digest with greater capacity the fruits of Mother Earth. And gently, over time, I felt myself coming back to the land of the living. I was blessed to find a new sense of community with my fellow brothers and sisters in a way that had been lacking during my time of isolation and illness. She was right, that goddess-priestess of my dreams. Plus, she had it all in the perfect order.

I am thankful for my experiences of awakening, and there has been no turning back. Even though my times of luminous awakening dance between phases of temporary sleepwalking and shadows of forgetting the truth, I am always graced with ample opportunities to remember once again. Each awakening continues to carry with it such a bright light of beauty, because the only thing we are ever truly waking up to is perfect love. Rise and shine!

Beauty tips for awakening

1. What is your story of awakening? What dream of fear in your life do you feel you need to awaken from? How might you express your awakening journey in words, a painting, a dance, a dish you prepare, a sculpture you form, or in whatever creative endeavour calls out to you from the depths of your soul?

2. Take a moment to recall some of the peak experiences in your life when you felt most awake. When were they? Where were you? Who were you with? How did you *feel*? Enjoy a few deep inhalations and exhalations, savouring

and giving thanks for those moments that still live on in your cellular memory. As you do this, you open the gateway for more of these beautiful moments to grace your life.

3. Practice awakening. When tempted to give in to the dream of fear in one aspect of your life today, choose to awaken to love instead. Example: If someone hurts or attacks you in some way, big or small, how can you perceive them and the situation differently? How can you awaken love rather than giving in to the unconscious conditioned response of fear? Notice which perception feels better to you: the fearful or the loving, the judgmental or the compassionate, the angry or the centred response? Awakening is possible in every single moment, in every conscious breath, in every beat of your pulsing heart.

4. Tomorrow morning, be aware (as an objective witness) of how you wake up from sleep. Do you get up with a jolt following a blaring alarm, unconsciously and robotically feeling pushed into life? Do you slowly and gently move from sleep to a wakened state with a big luscious stretch, tenderly entering into the day? How is your manner of waking up from sleep in the morning similar to your general way of doing your life? Something interesting to ponder. And remember, you can always practice waking up in a way that feels good, honouring who you are, where you're at, and whatever reality you long to create in this life.

Chapter 2

The Beauty Of Joy

"Live in joy, in love
Even among those who hate.
Live in joy, in health,
Even among the afflicted.
Live in joy, in peace,
Even among the troubled.
The winner sows hatred because the loser suffers.
Let go of winning and losing, and find joy."
Buddha

"Scatter joy."
Ralph Waldo Emerson

Defining joy

Joy is sexy. True joy, that is. Grounded joy. Deep joy. Unconditional joy. Is there any other kind? I think there is a temporal sense of happiness that is mistaken for joy. However, joy is not true joy until it emanates from the inner recesses of your soul and can't help but rise to the surface in a soft, knowing smile that is graciously contagious and not easily shaken. Sometimes favourable conditions help to bring out this joy, but I have also seen and experienced it in the midst of great struggle, when reasons for joy seem far, far away.

It is this joy that is beyond any judgment of good or bad, right or wrong, pleasure or pain. It is an infinite inner well of contentment, stemming from a deep and unquestioning sense of trust in life herself, which leads to a blissful state of being that sings, "God is good and all is well and life is beautiful." How would you like to awaken every morning and find rest every evening with that joyful mantra running through your head, guiding the way you live and move in the world? You can. Joy is always one deep breath and one truthful thought away.

Buddha-full joy

The first quote at the beginning of this chapter is offered to us by the awakened one himself, the Buddha, and the way it revealed its liberating wisdom in my life felt nothing less than miraculous. It was summertime, and my mother was in the depths of despair. Having struggled with depression for a couple of years, she had lost the will to live and reminded me of that very sad thought multiple times daily. Things had gotten so bad and out of control that she requested to be taken to a residential hospital specializing in mental health and addictions. We, her family and friends, all hoped and prayed that there she might get the help she needed in order to reignite her once vibrant spirit and return to the land of the living.

I was the one to stay at the family home, looking after my mother's basic affairs and taking turns with my sister visiting her as much as I could while working and preparing to move to the west coast of Canada to begin a master's degree in transpersonal psychology. My concerns about my mother's condition hung over me like a thick, dark, impenetrable cloud; to experience joy in any way felt like some horrible violation of her deep sadness. Yet, a part of me naturally longed for respite from the heaviness of her despair and for some spark of hope and happiness to be restored within me. Otherwise, would I have to wait until she was happy again to be happy, too?

One day, feeling stressed by it all and realizing the toll being taken on my body, health, and energy, I decided to book a Zen Shiatsu massage for myself. I thought that maybe this would ease some of my tension and bring greater energy flow to my meridians long enough for me to taste a bit of peace. Most of all, it was a vital act of self-love in the middle of the dramatic crisis going on around and within me. My mind was full of racing thoughts—scattered, foggy, and out of control. My heart felt lead-heavy. My body was exhausted, drained of energy. My spirit seemed a little crushed, or maybe a lot crushed. And so, from a weakened state as I was getting ready for the massage, I prayed for a ray of light to pierce through what felt like dense darkness.

When I began to get changed in preparation for the treatment, my eyes were magnetically drawn to a wall panel with this exquisitely perfect quote by the Buddha—the command to live in *joy* no matter what circumstance surrounds us. It was like a divine prescription or permission slip, giving me the ability to reclaim my joy and realize that to withhold it from myself was also to withhold it from all others. In that moment, I remembered how deeply connected my mom and me were, and I knew that if I gave in to sacrificing my joy until she found her joy again, we were both in big trouble. I no longer felt that it was a violation to experience my joy, but rather it was my divine responsibility to nourish my joy in service of my healing and hers. My sense of inner, unconditional joy and trust in the benevolence of the universe then became my cherished life-preserver in the midst of the stormy sea of my mother's depression, which would continue to swell for many months to come. I could breathe a little easier from that moment on. However, having copied down the quote for future reference, I reread it time and again as a helpful reminder.

A Course in Miracles states that joy has no cost and that it is our sacred birthright. So why do so many people look sad and forlorn? Have they all forgotten what is rightfully theirs to enjoy and share? Possibly, but all is not lost. I remember being on a public bus in Toronto a few years back. Having travelled already for about a half-hour in this vehicle filled with people who looked mostly dead, there was one woman seated directly in front of me with this big, wide grin gracing her beautiful face. She seemed to glow a soft and golden light amidst a whole lot of gray. There was a grace about her, an inner sense of calm and gladness that didn't look like it was going away any time soon. I looked at the book she was reading, and although I don't remember the exact title, the essence of it involved cultivating joy.

This anonymous woman on the bus looked like she was one of the people least in need of reading this material, and yet obviously by focusing her thoughts and intentions in the direction of joy, she was living and radiating it. I had no idea who she was or what her story entailed; to an outside observer, it seemed that she must have led a charmed life in order to be smiling in such a way. But in reality, she probably lived with as many (if not more) struggles and challenges as the rest of us, yet she chose to live in joy anyway. In that brief moment and small, wordless encounter, I felt how much her presence on this earth was a gift, and that her vibration of joy was calling me and all others to experience the same. I smiled at her and she smiled back, a knowing smile that was like joy recognizing itself and the universal love of humanity being shared. I suddenly saw public transportation in a whole new light. Literally.

Living joy

Two inspirational figures immediately come to mind when I consider what it means to live the beauty of joy—one from a few hundred years ago based in the mystical Christian tradition, and the other a modern phenomenon that is just too wonderful not to share with you. The first is Brother Lawrence, a monk who, in 17th century France, had his inspired thoughts put to paper and whose guidelines for a joy-filled life have been read by thousands if not millions of people since that time. Before joining the monastery, Brother Lawrence was a soldier in the Thirty-Year War where he became crippled due to a sciatic nerve injury that left him in chronic pain throughout his life. Upon joining the order, he began to serve as a humble cook in a newly established monastery, and for many years he grew and evolved in his community of faith. What lives on beyond his physical existence on this earth is the message he shares through his book, *The Practice of the Presence of God*: that the essence of the presence of the Most High is *joy*, and that communing with God is a conscious practice rather than a passive experience.

It was Brother Lawrence's opinion that "we should feed and nourish our soul with high notions of God which would yield us great joy in being devoted" (First Conversation). In every little activity and thought of every day, joy is the sure way to bring God into every aspect of one's life. According to the Brother, if joy is not in some way present, one is missing out on allowing the Divine to infiltrate even the most common and ordinary parts of human life, such as, in his case, cooking a meal or repairing a sandal. Work and prayer were one to him, as he possessed a great tranquility that permeated every aspect of his life in equal measure in his deep love for God and in God's deep love for him (Fourth Conversation). I love this idea. It reminds us that joy is a conscious choice and a very real possibility that we have the right to enjoy (in-joy!) at all times rather than being merely a fleeting feeling when things are going well. I find it highly comforting to be reminded that joy runs through our spirits as unquestionably as blood flows through our veins, and we can tap into that infinite supply whenever we choose to. And I am compelled as well to remember that even when sorrow, joy's twin, is in our midst, there is always a trace, a spark of joy dwelling in the vicinity, waiting to be practiced, longing to shine its gracious, sacred light.

And now we skip forward a few hundred years to the present, where there is Matt Harding. You might have heard of Matt from his infamous website, www.wherethehellismatt.com, or from seeing him on YouTube. And if you don't know of Matt yet, I'm happy to fill you in on his modern, global, joy-scattering phenomenon. Matt was a video game programmer in the United States who decided, at age twenty six, that he was not as fulfilled as he hoped he would be, and that he didn't want to spend the majority of his life staring at a computer screen and getting fat. He decided to take the money from his savings and travel the world for six months, not knowing necessarily what he would do or where his experiences might lead him. Matt says in an online PayScale interview that the hardest thing to do was to take that leap out of his comfort zone, leave the safety net he knew, and venture out and do something he really didn't know how to do. And yet, once he did, he realised that "the world really isn't as dangerous as it's made out to be." What a beautiful realisation.

What does all of this have to do with joy? Well, Matt has a little dance he likes to do that he and a co-worker used to call his "bad dance." He shifts his weight in a funky rhythm from side to side while his upper body finds some kind of synchronicity with his lower body, a big goofy smile gracing his face all the while. He would do this dance while he hovered over his friend's desk waiting for him to go for lunch. This same co-worker was traveling with Matt in Hanoi, and at one point while they had some time on their hands, he encouraged Matt to do his "bad dance" while he videotaped him. It was funny to them, so he kept dancing while being filmed in the many parts of the world he was visiting, and posted these videos on his website. Soon there were a couple of million downloads on his site because people were overjoyed to witness this unique phenomenon—a young man dancing "badly" all around the world in different landscapes and surrounded by people of all different ages, races, classes, creeds, and customs. Joy knows no limits or boundaries.

Things started snowballing from that point. In the year following his first round of global adventures, Matt was contacted by the Stride Gum company, an innovative and forward-thinking organization that proposed paying Matt to travel for another six months, money being no obstacle, being filmed doing his dance in even more parts of the world as a promotion of their product. Although Matt didn't start out with the intention of dancing "badly" all over the world, suddenly he was graced with an opportunity to travel 100,000 miles in six months and to spread joy through dancing everywhere he went. How fantastic is that?! How can one ever prepare oneself to have the doors open to that kind of experience? Matt shares that his favourite clip is from Mulindi, Rwanda, where he began to dance and kids flooded in to join him from all over the town, wanting to dance, too. He states that this amazing moment created an "immediate access to joy," and you can feel it all through your being when you watch this part of the video covering his world-wide dance fest. One of the greatest messages Matt brings from this whole experience is that often we limit our options or allow others to limit our possibilities, and we live within self-created walls for our existence. It is a major shift to realize that you're the one creating or accepting those boundaries, and that you actually have control over changing them if you so choose.

This awareness can lead to a new sense of freedom and liberation within a joy-filled life where all things are truly possible. No one outside of us has the right or power to squelch our joy. And so, we must be diligent in protecting and nourishing our inner joy on a moment-to-moment basis. We each have the power to find our own unique ways of connecting with that infinite well of joy residing within us. Become intimately connected with yours. Certain people in our lives can also help us to tap into our true joy, and the times we share with them allow our joy to surface from the depths. My young nieces, Stephanie and Natalie, have both been an incredible joy to me since the moment they were born. It is rare for me to spend time with them without coming away deeply in touch with my inner joy. I am constantly challenged to renew and nourish my joy when I start to forget that it is waiting and available to be celebrated on a daily basis. Each one of us must be on a mission to scatter joy in our daily lives. Who can think of a more beautiful way to live?

Beauty tips for joy

1. Recall a time when you felt happiness and another time when you felt joy. What was the difference? Do your best to explore and express those subtle and not-so-subtle differences. Try to recall your joy specifically and as accurately as possible, using all your senses so that you get intimately acquainted with it.

2. If joy is forever living inside you, waiting to be acknowledged and expressed, what is holding you back right here and right now from being joyful? What are your personal "joy-snatchers"? What are your core beliefs about joy? Which beliefs limit you and which beliefs liberate you?

3. If you were to take yourself on a joy-date, doing something that absolutely delights you, what would you do? Where would you go? Who would join you? *Do it*. For real.

4. Giving and receiving are one in truth, and therefore as we bring joy to another, we awaken the joy within us. What tangible thing can you do or say today that you know will awaken the sleeping joy in someone you love? There is always something. Whatever it is, go for it. And watch how the joy magically expands and multiplies. If you are forever waiting for someone else to bring you joy, you are missing the whole point. *Be* the joy-scatterer and the fullness of joy is already yours.

Chapter 3

The Beauty Of Change

"It has often been said that the only unchanging thing in the world is change itself. Life is continuously changing, evolving, dying, and being reborn."

Osho Zen Tarot

"The river where you set your foot just now is gone—those waters give way to this, now this."

Heraclitus

Nature of change

To resist change is akin to resisting the breath; it is essential to life itself. Despite our conscious desire or will, the earth, our home, spins methodically in a well-ordered, complex galaxy, and our personal worlds are microcosmic reflections of our larger universe. It is amazing to simply ponder this reality. It is only natural that there are times when we desperately long for change, such as when the going gets tough and the dark tunnel seems endless and without any glimmer of light. In these moments, when it seems life could not get any worse, change represents a beacon of hope, signaling the opportunity for things to shift into something a little better or easier. And it is equally natural that at other times, when our happiness is so full that we can hardly contain it—such as moments of feeling utterly in love, that the world is our oyster and we its pearl, when we are in full agreement with the popular saying "Life is Good"—change might be the last thing we are seeking. In such sweet instances, we just want the world to stop and keep us forever enjoying those moments of total bliss. No such luck.

The Buddha explored the nature of change in great depth. He utilized this in teaching the rest of us how to attain a greater capacity for peace in the midst of life's many shades and textures of suffering. One of the foundational Buddhist doctrines affirms the reality of impermanence, with the very essence of life being characterized by flux and fluidity. Our bodies reflect this truth: our cells and tissues are forever dying and being reborn, creating entirely new beings every seven years. Deepak Chopra is a modern scientist and mystic who explains this miraculous phenomenon in detail, asserting that one's consciousness is in charge of the creation and evolution of the physical body, temporarily inhabited by a spirit. He states it brilliantly in his book *Perfect Health* with these words: "The secret of life… is that anything in your body can be changed with the flick of an intention." Can you imagine? It takes just a flick. The potential for change in a system of constant renewal is therefore limitless. So what are we waiting for? It is up to us to use this powerful information to our highest advantage, both for our own personal healing and for the greater common good.

I have been a keen witness to both my own futile resistance to change and that of people surrounding me. In all such cases, the suffering has been epic. In my conditioning as a child, I felt that I needed to be perfect in order to be loved and accepted. I took this understanding to its most basic physical level, as many young girls do, resulting far too often in debilitating eating disorders accompanied by a distorted sense of self-esteem. My sense of self during my mid-teens and early twenties became mostly material and superficial, regardless of my spiritual and essential value. I tried to do everything in my power and control to look perfect. In my longing to be loved and accepted, I assumed that I needed to be beautiful according to the latest cultural standards: flawless complexion, thin body, and tall stature. At the same time, I needed to be brilliant and successful in school and outside activities, popular in my social circle, and moving toward a successful professional career and prosperous life path that would dazzle my family and make them proud. No pressure at all!

As a result, my obsessive, controlling attempts to conform to some illusory image of perfection had me starving and sick in body, mind, and soul. Whenever I felt close to this physical ideal, I could feel myself holding my breath. I thought I would only be loved when physically perfect, so I didn't want anything to change; just like that—freeze frame. I was a prisoner within the cold, rigid grips of my own fear and mistaken beliefs, a lonely and crazy way to live.

Change that heals

With a history of compromised immune function due to the parasites and CFS, as well as the eating disorder I developed during those years, it took much divine healing to change my heart and mind, to wake me up from this nightmare that had taken over my whole being. I realized through my resistance to change and the suffering this created that the way I was living really wasn't working. Little by little, I needed to surrender to the flow of life instead of using all my energy to defend against it. I needed to nourish myself with positive thoughts, the loving warmth of blessed friends, healthy food, and spiritual truths of innate rather than superficial perfection. Fortunately, I regained a right relationship with my body as an organic temple and instrument of the Holy Spirit of God rather than as an ornament, solely valued for its external appearance. I needed to accept, embrace, and dive wholeheartedly into this change in order to let go and heal. What I found was not the loss of love and approval as I feared, but rather the most authentic experience of love I have ever known, deeply rooted in a compassionate sense of mystery and grace rather than in the empty promises of control and supposed perfection.

And so, here I am, many moons later and many years wiser, on much more sane and solid ground, having had the heartbreaking experience of holding my mother in my arms as she collapsed under the weight of her depression. She found herself re-living patterns of abandonment and betrayal in intimate relationships, and her spirit was crushed from all of the suffering. I saw in the depths of her pain a similar resistance to the one I had once held to the natural course of change in life, and I could only hope that my own successful evolution could be of some inspiration to her worn and weary spirit. The pain-filled words that came from her mouth time and time again screamed of desperation and a stubborn unwillingness to move into newness:

"I'd rather die than change," "I can't do this. It's too hard. I'm not going to make it," "Help me!"

I wavered between the weighty burden of needing to save her somehow (despite knowing better than that) and throwing my hands up in the air, feeling powerless to do anything but love her as best I could through this deep, dark journey. This latter stance was actually the most powerful one I could adopt. During her times of threatening suicide, I didn't know which path her soul would choose as she faced the stark crossroads between life and death, but I did have the power to honor her personal path—one that I knew I had no control over. I could only respect the choices she made as she stumbled along her journey as she yearned longingly for some ray of light to pierce through the thick clouds of her perpetual gloom.

Don't get me wrong, it felt nearly impossible to not try and take over and find some way to convince her to not give up. There were so many times that I wished she would choose one or the other—life or death—and just get on with it, because this stagnant, perpetual in-between place felt worse than anything. Of course, I had no desire for my mother to die; I just didn't know how long I could stand to witness her living a life-less life. One day when she said to me, for the umpteenth time, that she was ready to end it all, I decided it was time to change my strategy and practice radical acceptance. Instead of going into my usual pro-life speech, attempting desperately to say the magic words that might spark some motivation and enthusiasm back into her, I simply looked deep into her eyes and calmly said, "Okay."

She freaked out. "Okay? *Okay*?! So you don't care if I die?"

"No, that's not it at all, Mom. Of course I want you to live. I just can't be the one to fight for your life anymore, and whatever you choose to do, I love you," I replied as steadily as I could.

Whoosh. This whole exchange was painful and difficult, yet amazingly liberating at the same time. It was actually a big turning point that changed our relationship, on some level empowering us both. Codependency is never effective. My accepting her unconditionally and not taking responsibility for her healing helped to shift the responsibility back into her court. I believe that it was one of the factors that helped her to eventually come to the powerful and sobering realisation that her life was truly in her hands—for better or for worse.

Fashionable change

One of the most fitting metaphors regarding change came to me through something my exquisitely and almost obsessively fashion-conscious mother could totally relate to: clothing. As my mother and I drove home together one day, I silently asked God to aid me in finding the words to help her understand how vital it was that she "let go" into life again. On a cold autumn day leading into the chill of winter, we were having yet another conversation about the necessity for change in her life. Suddenly, a spark of wisdom inspired me.

"Mom, you wouldn't wear a light summer dress on a winter's day, would you? When the season changes, you need to adjust your wardrobe accordingly, right? If you went out in sandals and that short dress on a day like today, you'd totally freeze! It's the same way with life. We need to adapt and change our ways if we are to thrive in the environment of *today*."

She seemed to get the message; however it didn't register sufficiently for her to be willing to immediately take off that cherished summer dress and exchange it for some nice wool pants and a cozy sweater. In that moment, she still chose to live in the stale and lifeless atmosphere of the past and continued hanging on to self-pity for dear life. She would rather continue to freeze than put on the appropriate clothing. Her fear of letting go of the past and stepping into a present and a future that overwhelmed her was so big that she would still rather die than change. And thus her life looked more like death than life at that time. I say that without judgment and with a lot of compassion, because at times my life has looked pretty much the same.

What is it about change that scares us to death instead of drawing us deeper into life? I believe it is the foreign aura of the distrusted unknown. Even if the present is horribly sad, depressing, and dark, it becomes comfortable in its familiarity. We know it. We trust it. We feel safe in it, even if we are miserable. A wise friend eloquently expressed how I now feel about the process of change. We were discussing what was going on with my mother and what happens for so many people who get stuck when he asked with sincerity and compassion, "Does she have *any* idea how beautiful it is on the other side?" No, she must not. Otherwise she would be spurred on to new life. She would let go into the great river of life, which is always replenished, flowing, and changing, making its way around obstacles and ultimately back to source. She wouldn't cling steadfastly to the rocks on the shoreline, too afraid of what might come next.

What does it take for us to trust the flow of change that is at the very core of existence on this planet? I believe it requires the gift of an inner vision of what *can* be granted to each of us by the sheer grace of the Divine. Somewhere deep inside, perhaps due to the spark of life we each carry in our sacred hearts, lies the seed of hope, the possibility of faith, and the assurance of essential goodness. What does it take for each of us to unearth this buried treasure? That is the mystery I abandon myself to daily as I give great thanks for the changes that have blessed, and continue to enhance, my fluid and beautiful life. There was a subway advertisement at one time that my eyes were always drawn to that felt reassuring in its blunt simplicity. It read "Change is good." It really does help to believe that.

Change + acceptance = inner peace

"Anitya, anitya, anitya." Chanting these words marks the beginning of the Buddhist meditative practice of Vipassana, which is also known as Insight Meditation. I was first introduced to this powerful practice through my acquaintance with a few people in my Religious Studies classes at McGill University who had attended at least one, if not many, of the ten-day intensive courses at a Vipassana retreat center. There was something about those who had practiced this style of meditation that attracted me. They seemed to have a steady, solid peace and poise about them, a sense of awakened and highly embodied presence. There was something in their eyes that deeply and mysteriously shared their ability to be fully accepting, observant, and non-resistant to the vicissitudes in life, which inevitably brought them a rich sense of serenity.

An ex-boyfriend of mine had attended a Vipassana retreat in Quebec shortly after one of our many break-ups. He shared with me later that the suffering that was triggered by our on-again, off-again relationship was perfect grist for his mill during those long ten days. He had the chance to deeply observe the crazy dynamics of his mind and also to liberate himself through the meditative practice. He had me intrigued, to say the least. So eventually, I accompanied a dear friend of mine, Janet, to Massachusetts to dive into my own Vipassana experience.

I had been duly warned—it was a very strict environment in terms of how purely you are to devote yourself to the mind training. You are to bring absolutely no reading or writing material; you eat the food offered by those gracious enough to provide for you from a previous training. As soon as the ten-day session begins, you commit to having no contact with others in the group. You are to be solely and completely with your own being—mind, body, and soul—while allowing the Vipassana meditation to do its work, which was aptly called "psychic surgery" by one of the group leaders.

Janet assumed that I would breeze through the experience because I had done a great deal of yoga, meditation, and personal growth work over the years. Meanwhile, she was afraid that the training might be a living hell for her, since she had a history of agoraphobia and panic attacks and was concerned about what might come up in the duration. I didn't really know what to expect, but I felt ready for it. Was I ever in for a surprise. As destiny would have it, Janet had the good fortune to receive a private room on the main floor with a lovely window overlooking the garden. I was offered either a shared tent, which upon inspection felt like a small, enclosed sauna, or a cool basement room shared with two other women. I chose the latter option. Little did I know that this would be merely the beginning of my opportunities to witness my sense of resistance and repulsion. I could either suffer with my negative mind or surrender to things just as they were and find some semblance of peace.

The two women I roomed with, who I'm quite sure are incredibly lovely individuals, created some of the most awful, disgusting, repulsive bodily noises I have ever heard in my life. I'm not exaggerating; burping, farting, hoarking, snoring, you name it, if it was loud and unendurable, it was part of the soundtrack of my ten days of training. In addition, rather than breezing through the experience, the practice of sitting with myself twenty-four/seven brought up such pain and intense suffering that I desperately wanted to leave by day three. I even created a "busting-out" plan: I would sneak into the car of a woman who left at about 3:00 p.m. every day. I would hide in the backseat and make my getaway as soon as she parked somewhere out of sight and sound of the center. I would deal with how to rejoin Janet later. I needed to get back to everyday civilisation and some version of my normal life that was full of potential distractions, and fast! It is amazing what schemes the fear-based ego mind will cook up when it feels highly threatened.

But back to what this has to do with change. The Vipassana meditation training is all about having insight into that which causes us to suffer—mainly our grasping after what is not and resisting that which is. Both of those nasty tricks of the mind steal any possibility of peace and happiness, taking us away from the gifts and blessings of the present moment. By being highly aware and observant of our physical body, doing a neutral and systematic inner scan of sensations from head to toe and back up through the body again, we begin to be able to sit without judgment or preference (ideally!) as we subtly notice, with an equal mind and heart, both the pleasures and pains we feel. Once we can do this with physical sensations, it becomes much easier to extend the practice to all aspects of our lives, and thus to cultivate an adamantine peace that remains unperturbed by the many facets of life's impermanence.

When change occurs, we don't resist it or grasp after something different. We come to accept and embrace all that is, just as it is, and just as it was, and just as it will be. The freedom resulting from that awakened inner stance is exquisitely blissful, and well worth the endurance and perseverance to complete the training and to practice cultivating this insight in one's everyday life. I moved as gently and compassionately as I could through the challenges that each day presented. Mind you, those days often seemed like weeks, months, and even years at times. In the end, having stayed the course and given the process a chance to work its magic, I now enjoy this meditative practice and see it as a godsend in my life due to the tremendous peace it brings me. I am so grateful that I didn't make my getaway on day three.

Beauty tips for change

1. "Anitya, anitya, anitya." Awareness, acceptance, awakening. The winds of change will always blow— how are you meeting them at this point in your life? What kind of dance are you doing with the changes that are calling out to you?

2. Which season of change are you in now? Is it a time of spring-filled rebirth? Are you experiencing a warm and easy summertime vibe? Is life leading you to accept a letting-go autumnal energy? Are you in a hibernating, inner focused wintry phase? What is your relationship to this particular season of change? What would you like it to be?

3. I suggest taking a deep breath. With every inhalation, allow the changes of life to gently caress your skin like a soft breeze and enter into every cell of your being. With every exhalation, release a layer of resistance you are holding onto in the face of change. Notice how you feel. Breathe the peace. Notice your aliveness. You are an integral and precious part of the ever-changing process of life.

4. How does your life look and feel when you actually *embrace* and *engage* with the changes in your life instead of resisting and denying them? What if you made friends with change instead of wasting so much time in resistance? How would that feel? How would your life *change*?

Part II:

Honouring the Beauty of the South

We turn our awakening hearts to the South and we give great thanks for:
Warm days and soft nights that allow the soul to find sweet rest
Fullness of abundance
Sharing with friends and family in holiday adventures
Campfires and bonfires and nights of star-gazing
Mother Earth offering her whole body for our nourishment and enjoyment
Summer love
A hundred billion night-sky stars
Sand beneath our feet and fresh dips in the water
Camping and retreating into nature for replenishment
Heat and life at its peak
Sunshine and rain
Animals awake and alive
Fulfillment of dreams and dreaming new dreams
Softly watching the night come
HO!

Chapter 4

The Beauty of Love

"God is but love, and therefore so am I."
Dr. Helen Schucman, A Course in Miracles

"If I am without love, I am nothing ... Love never comes to an end."
1 Corinthians 13:2, 8

"When love beckons to you, follow him,
Though his ways are hard and steep.
And when his wings enfold you, yield to him,
Though the sword hidden among his pinions may wound you."
Kahlil Gibran

Fear of love

Love is the most sought-after, indefinable, and feared experience in this crazy yet beautiful human existence. Why do I include fear? Because we say we want love, but then when it shows up—raw, real, and rocking our world—we tend to put on our best runners and head for the hills. Love is the most basic human quality of goodness, kindness, tenderness, and graciousness, and when it gets deep in our cells, it searches out our wounds to heal them. But sometimes this can feel painful initially and we resist it with everything we've got.

Fortunately, there is a purity about true love that makes us willing to do anything and everything to move through the resistance to it so that love can heal our wounds rather than re-wound us.

The most universal expression of love that I have seen, which reminds me that in essence we truly *are* all one, comes in the form of a smile. Every time a stranger or loved one smiles at me, I am reminded that a smile is quite simply the facial equivalent to love. I have a feeling that even before we are born, when we are a developing fetus in our mother's womb, we are tiny beings of pure love expressing the primal essence of human existence in the natural state of balanced giving and receiving. This remains true throughout the course of our lives, yet most of us tend to forget this essential fact early on—possibly even as the great force of life pushes us through the birth canal and we enter this cold, bright, strange, painful, and wonderful world.

I remember when as a young child I looked to my family for basic love and approval, I knew when I was getting it and when I wasn't. The withdrawal of love when I did something that drew disapproval felt like a vast and gaping black hole of death, and so, good little girl that I was (or wanted to be, whichever was the case in the moment), I learned very quickly how to act in order to receive the most love possible. For me, the love and approval of my family constituted the most important thing in this world; if I needed to censor or adjust my behaviour in order to get it, I did whatever it took.

The big problem with this approval-seeking dynamic is that when we begin to live in such an externally referenced and disempowering manner, we tend to give up pieces of ourselves in ways that make us forget who we really are. We self-amputate until limb by limb, piece by piece, we become smaller versions of who we really are. This is neither a good nor a loving thing, which is why once we realize what is happening, we usually spend the rest of our lives learning to restore love to ourselves again, reintegrating our lost parts, reclaiming bit by bit our magnificent, whole, wonderful selves. "To thine own self be true" is a classic gem of Shakespearean dictum. How to really do this authentically and consistently is the clincher.

An eloquent and masterful professor of Hindu studies at McGill University taught an ancient parable that serves as a wonderful reminder to love and accept ourselves just as we are, and to express ourselves and our gifts in this world to the greatest extent possible. It is the story of a man who seemed to live his life fully and successfully, forever emulating the great people around him and trying his best to be just like them. When he died and found himself standing before God, he expected to receive a celestial pat on the back for how wonderfully he had spent his time on earth. Instead, God looked at him with compassionate and inquisitive eyes, and said, "But why were you not *you*?" What a powerful and soul-shaking question. This man may have excelled at being a high-quality mosaic of a person, blending the best characteristics of many others, but he had not used his life energy to explore and express *himself,* his innate qualities, which was his true *dharma,* or purpose in this life.

Love is …

One of my earliest memories of learning about love came from the fridge of my first home. Not the fridge itself, mind you, but a fridge magnet with a cute caricature of a grinning little girl with the words "Love is …" above her head. Below her lay the answer, "… giving and forgiving." I was too young to understand what that meant, although in an unselfconscious way I was already part of the universal flow of giving and receiving—receiving nourishment and love and giving it back in my own instinctual childish ways. But forgiving? What did that mean? I had no idea what it was or why it would ever be necessary. The closest thing I might have witnessed as forgiveness involved an event that occurred in the very kitchen that was home to the fridge with the magnet on it.

I'm not sure if I remember this event because it was the first time I was hoisted up to the sink to help with the dishes, or because of the hilarity of the moment. I have no memory of the circumstances leading to this particular situation, but the whipped cream meant to adorn our dinner's dessert ended up flying back and forth between my mother and father in a chaotic scene of much laughter as the sweet, white, fluffy mush was squirted and thrown by my normally calm, rational parents. I remember my sister and me gleefully witnessing the whole event, sitting in utter shock when the whipped-cream fight ended abruptly and the laughter turned to tension. My mom was the first to stop laughing. She became very upset that my father had ruined her new hairstyle and sharply ordered us all to clean up.

The love between my parents was being challenged by a sort of conflict that ended up in a food-flinging fight that produced some obvious hard feelings. As I put my small hands to the task of cleaning up, for the first time I had an inkling of something not being okay, of some balance having been overthrown, of something needing to be set right. Love in the form of giving and forgiving was required to make things right again. This is such a trifling example, and yet the teachings of A Course in Miracles states that each call for forgiveness is of equal weight, and that there is no order of difficulty in miracles.

Even if we want to separate one instance of conflict from another because it seems more grave or harmful, the essence of the miracle is always the shift from fear to love, and it is equally effective and powerful. Always. I don't remember how things got resolved between my parents that night, but I do know that this was just one example of the many calls for love that characterise all relationships.

As I ponder love, there are so many things I can share about its true beauty that abide both in its light and sweetness as well as in its shadow side, its bitter sting. Some deep and powerful lifelong loves are undeniable in their fated beginnings and grow over time; those consistent relationships that are consciously nurtured with tenderness, patience, and unyielding dedication, even in the face of great resistance and struggle. Often these are family bonds, which many current spiritual teachers suggest we choose before we are born on this planet because we have soul lessons to learn with these people. Especially if our family relations are challenging, this thought can often leave us shaking our heads as we move through life because we have no idea what we must have been thinking at the time. These loves inevitably have much to teach us. Even if we try to turn away from them, they seem to always come back and stare us in the face, offering us opportunities for growth as we rise to the occasion of nourishing the current of that love rather than shutting off the love-tap.

Some great loves show up in our lives unannounced—intimate connections that passionately and graciously reveal themselves in a splendor that takes our breath away. These loves tend to make us blissfully happy to be alive, even if there will be pain in the eventual parting from this particular "Big Love." And of course, we can't forget the tough loves, which we often would rather not call "loves," that try our patience, test our will, drive us to hell and back, and then send us the bill. These relationships remind us, whether we like it or not, that some of our greatest teachers in this life can show up in strange and unidentifiable disguises. Perhaps there are as many kinds of love as there are different kinds of people, yet the essence of love remains the same: a beautiful expression of the tender heart that longs to intimately know itself and to be known—beyond definition, limitation, or control in any way, shape, or form.

Ultimately, we have so much to learn from all the relationships in our life, and love-school never ends. A popular saying in Bali, shared with me by a dear friend who spent much time there, sums up that which is essential in this life. It has to do with the three questions we are all called to ask ourselves at the end of our life on earth as we know it: How well did you live? How well did you love? How well did you learn to let go? The answers to these questions reveal the quality of the life lived, the love shared, and the ability to surrender control even in the face of great fears.

Big loves

When we talk of our "love life," we all know what we mean: those intimate partnerships that promise the ecstasy of heaven and often put us through the purifying fires of hell. I have grown powerfully through my intimate relationships, which have tested me right to the core as I faced my harshest resistances and my deepest wounds and fears. These loves have graciously offered me amazing beauty and tenderness in the vulnerable, fluid, mutual sharing of love. My first real and intense experience of falling in love and growing through love occurred when I was sixteen years old.

I had met the young man at a summer camp where we both were guests and staff at various points in our teenage years. He had a reputation for being a "bad boy," and yet he seemed so good to me when I first laid eyes on him but didn't yet have the courage to explore anything more than a distant crush. Even though he had gotten a bad rap in the past, he was in the process of trying to redeem himself when I met up with him for the second time. I had just finished a two-month health protocol of various herbal remedies to try and rid my body of the Giardia parasites that had made me sick for three years, and I was very hopeful that much health and happiness lay ahead in my not-too-distant future. My life and his life were both looking up, and it felt like a sweet twist of fate that we were brought together again.

I sat on the couch next to him during a camp Bible study. I have no idea what the topic of discussion was that night because all I can recall was my rapidly beating heart, my awareness of his body so close to mine, and the excitement of our shared passion for the spiritual path. If this love was going to develop, our mutual love for God was going to be its center. That was our intention, anyway. We both must have been aware of the untapped chemistry sparking between us as we continued to attend Bible studies together and allowed this energy to build in an exciting yet unexplored way.

Finally, after a couple of weeks of playful flirtation, we made our first official date—he would come to my home and I would make us lunch. The night before he was to come over, I couldn't sleep because I felt my body vibrating and stirring in a manner totally foreign to me but highly welcome; a heated anticipation of all that was to come, perhaps—all the karma we would live out together. He ended up being quite late for lunch, which worried me a bit, but he did eventually make it, showing up with a huge gift basket as a peace offering. The big romance had begun, and it would take many twists, turns, slides, leaps, and tumbles over the year and a half we were together.

This was my first exuberant love experience, and as is common for first loves, none other can compare. I was enraptured and willing to do anything for him and with him. Life became magical again, and opening up to our love was a real awakening of my sensuality, sexuality, and desires as a quite naïve and impressionable young woman. Still working to shed his "bad boy" image, he enrolled in the local Bible college to explore his spiritual leanings and aspirations. He was gorgeous, charming, charismatic, brilliant in every way, and determined to use his gifts for the greater good. Who wouldn't fall madly in love with all *that*?

We gave each other the best and brightest of ourselves. Then, as often happens with beloveds as the months pass and the unresolved subconscious dynamics surface, we began to dance with one another's demons. He became insanely jealous if I even so much as looked too friendly with a waiter serving us, and wanted to know if another man ever entered my thoughts or dreams. He wouldn't even permit me to visit my grandparents in a neighboring town for fear that I might betray him. As for me, my hopes for health and happiness were snuffed out rather quickly when I developed CFS shortly after we began dating. It was so frustrating and challenging for me to be sick *again*, and so I tried to push him away by using various techniques of withdrawal and self-pity. I do believe we really loved each other. Yet, he had some major anger issues toward women that over time came out toward me, and I had some major fears about opening to love that got in the way. Ultimately, the intense fire of passion that brought us together gave us each first-degree love burns.

Ending our relationship was one of the hardest things I have ever done, because I truly believed we would have children and grow through all the phases of life with one another. But when I saw that I had begun to fear him more than I felt love for him, I knew I had to make a choice. I loved myself enough to let go of the relationship, even though I knew I would love him like no other in this life. I have no regrets when I think of what he and I shared, and yet I have had much healing work to do in order to build any kind of trust in men and in love after what happened between us.

His anger turned to violence, first toward walls and windows and then toward me. I was his angel and then all of a sudden I was the recipient of his uncontrollable rage. On some level, I think I knew it wasn't my fault, but at the time it didn't always feel so clear. I wondered how I attracted such abusive dynamics into my life; the rest of my family seemed so much healthier than me. Over the years it became clearer why he was my first love, because when I honestly explored what I believed about myself, I saw how he was a mirror for those hidden, messy, ugly, false beliefs that were lurking in my subconscious. I feared that in some way I was bad, guilty, not good enough. It was up to me to make some big-time corrections in my core belief system and to start living the truth, but it would take many years and short-lived intimate connections before I enjoyed the fruit of so much hard love-work.

Big Love Number Two didn't come around until about six years later after my first love and I had broken up. I was deeply jaded and afraid to let myself ever be so vulnerable again. Big, thick fortress walls of self-protection had been erected strategically around my heart, and to let them down and trust again seemed near impossible. There was also much loss that followed the end of that first relationship. My family fell apart just a year or so later, and shortly thereafter both of my grandfathers had heart attacks and passed away. Loss followed loss followed loss, and pain seemed to fill every corner and crevice of my heart. It is no wonder that it took six years for me to catch my love-breath.

Once again, love came into my life when I was in a phase of new beginnings, having just returned at age twenty five to McGill University in order to finish the Bachelor's Degree that I had started and then abandoned years earlier. My next boyfriend and I met at a Religious Studies faculty dinner. There was an immediate connection between us in our shared passion for Reiki, a powerful method of energy healing. I wasn't necessarily interested in him in a romantic way at first, but he says he had an eye for me from the very beginning. Excited about my new life, I said a sincere prayer one brisk autumn morning at the top of Mount Royal in Montreal, inviting into my life and heart a new angel-man for me to love and be loved by. I had just seen the movie *The City of Angels* with Meg Ryan and Nicolas Cage, and I humbly and sincerely put my prayerful order in for the bliss of such a beautiful connection (without the tragedy part, of course).

One thing I have learned is that when you invite something into your life, it's important to welcome the gift with gratitude and trust rather than with doubt and skepticism. At first, this man didn't seem to me like the one who would step into my life as my love-partner, and so I didn't allow myself to consider him as an option. Then the feelings grew strong and the draw toward him burned in me like a consistent fire. One night while we spoke on the phone, I got sweaty and nervous and couldn't resist opening up to the possibility of *us*. He sweetly acknowledged that he had a crush on me too. Thus began a three-year on-again-off-again love that delighted me to my core and also brought me to absolute panic when we got too close.

He was an amazing gift in my life. I asked for an angel, and I definitely got one. He was beautiful, generous, loving, caring, tender, passionate, and a lot of fun. Plus, he adored me. Our connection began with blessed exchanges of Reiki sessions and evolved into a kind of rollercoaster relationship, loving and witnessing each other through our university years—in his case, graduate work, and in mine, the completion of my bachelor's degree. What do I remember most when I think about this particular Big Love? I let myself go with the flow as best I could without freaking out (at times I totally lost it!) as we got to know each other and shared time in Montreal going to movies, attending lectures through the Religious Studies department, and enjoying nights at his place listening to music, cooking, and hanging out with his two lovely cats.

He often brought me flowers—luscious birds of paradise and big, bright sunflowers—and I bought him his favorite snacks and placed them lovingly in his mailbox. Reiki energy continued to flow through our connection, and he gave me one of the most precious gifts the last Christmas we were together: a huge glow-in-the-dark Reiki symbol to hang above my bed so that the healing energy would bless me constantly while I slept. I was deeply touched. There were times when my feelings and desire for him burned in me with a passion I couldn't explain or control. Love mixed with lust and tempered by a base of authentic friendship—a wild combination.

So it all sounds really great, wonderful, and all should be well in my world, right? In some ways, it *was* all good. *But,* I was scared out of my wits to truly unite with *anyone.* And in my mind, my crazy mind that was programmed rigidly to protect myself from all possible further pain (which is insane in and of itself because this mind creates the very pain it supposedly seeks to prevent), I was pretty convinced that even though this was a really good love in my life, it wasn't "it"—whatever that meant. My grandmother kept asking me if I was sure he wasn't "the one" for me. She really wanted me to find my mate, and in the wisdom of her years of life experience, she continued urging me to search the depths of my heart for my truth.

I loved him, I couldn't stand being apart from him, and yet I wouldn't totally let him in. When we got close physically and emotionally, which we did frequently, I went into full-fledged panic mode. I would wake up in the middle of the night and could hardly breathe. I was scared that I was making a mistake, and was convinced that I had to end things with him right away to become safe again. I vividly remember my heart beating rapidly, which prompted me to call him at about 3:00 a.m. to end our relationship, hoping this would ease my anxiety. However, my fear of opening to love would not go away just because I tried to push love away. So we went back and forth, and I drove him crazy with all my ups and downs and spiraling around. He was wonderful with me through it all, mostly steady, loving, and unbelievably patient. But he was still human and vulnerable and could only handle so much opening and closing with me before he couldn't take it anymore. As I consider his part in our relationship, I believe that he was there with me in that particular way at that specific point in time and space to learn his own lessons as well.

It boiled down to this: By the time we finished our education at McGill, I wanted to move back to Toronto and start a new life there with my family and friends as I was not at all ready for the sacred union he had envisioned for us. The thought of marrying him and having children together made me feel trapped, and there was still so much I wanted to experience in my life beyond Montreal, McGill University, and us. I convinced myself that this was for the best, and yet my heart ached. We said goodbye to one another, and as we left each other's presence, it was different than before. Usually when we walked away in opposite directions, we would both keep turning back every few seconds to glance at each other until we were out of each other's sight. It was one of our sweet rituals that spoke of our deep caring for one another.

However, on this day, even though I was the one who ended our relationship yet again, it was me who turned back first as a part of me still deeply longed to be with him. I waited and waited, but he never looked back. I kept watching until he was gone, hoping to witness even a slight angling of his head. But there was no movement in any direction except straight ahead for him. This was the moment I knew he was really done. I had pushed him away for the last time, and there was truly no going back for him after that, even if I tried. And oh, I tried.

After moving back to Toronto and dating other men, I realized how great I had it with him. I prayed for one more chance with this angel man. But it was truly too late. I cried so many tears for years, and I wondered if I'd ever get another chance to love and be loved by a man so wonderful. It was a deep sadness for me when I realized that my fear kept me from fulfilling this love in a way that could have been so complete, beautiful, and rich. But life is gracious and love is compassionate, and there are always more opportunities to heal and to love. Sometimes we are called to hold on, sometimes we are called to let go, and sometimes we must do both at the same time, even if that seems impossible.

As things came to an end between Big Love Number Two and me, I drew a picture that symbolized where I was in my life in relation to love and to what I had lived with him. It was our arms and hands reaching toward one another in the middle of a blood-red drop. Inside this drop were several green vines, leaves, and flowers. The image was full of life. However, although our hands reached toward one another, they didn't meet. Love was calling us together, but my fear kept us from fully uniting and walking through this life side by side. I will love him forever.

This was a very confusing and painful time for me. I knew I wanted love and knew I was pushing it away, but I felt unable to do anything different. I cried out to God for help. I wanted a simple and clear answer: Was he "the one," yes or no? If yes, I believed I could muster up enough courage to move through my fear and step deeper into love with him. If no, I would have the courage to really let go. I didn't get the clear answer I sought so desperately when I listened to the still, small voice of love inside me. What I did hear was this: "You choose, and I will go with you." No one could make this decision for me, and nothing, not even cataclysmic divine intervention, was going to save me from my muffled confusion. I had to learn this lesson myself, and the only clarity I gained was the knowledge that there was no black-and-white answer. Over the years I have come to accept the experience for what it was, grateful that I had the chance to enjoy at least a partial opening to love with this beautiful soul, even though, at that time, I found myself unable to sustain it.

Several years later, with many lessons learned, many layers of deep wounds healed, and having experienced many cycles of gentle heart openings and expansions, I find myself in one of the most intense, beautiful love relationships of my life. My partner is a man unlike anyone I've ever known. I remember the exact moment when I called him in. I had just bought the book *Soul Love* by Sanaya Roman, which is a type of channeled guidebook for opening up the energies of the heart and for connecting with our soul loves in this life—both intimate partnership and with those of the different circles of our soul tribe.

Sitting in quiet reflection, I read the book by candlelight and focused on the chapter regarding soul mates. I followed the instructions through a guided meditation to connect in essence with my soul mate. In that moment, in every cell of my being, I felt like I was joining, heart to heart, with the man I would share my life with, and in a very subtle but powerful way I could feel his beauty. A wave of happiness, trust, and certainty that we would somehow, somewhere, find one another washed over me, and I regained a sense of hope and lightness that allowed grace to reach me once again.

A few years later, I met my current partner and husband. We were enrolled in the same Yoga Teacher Training Course on the Pacific Coast of Costa Rica. At first we were simply friends, because neither of us was truly ready for the other just yet. One of the first things I remember noticing about my partner was his eyes— gorgeous ocean-blue eyes that seemed to contain the entire universe. Soulful. The second remembrance I have of him was his playfulness. He repeatedly invited me to leave the "safe" confines of the yoga training facility to explore a nearby beach, to which I kept saying, "No, thank you." And the third major memory of him during that magical time was his heart. I could see that his heart was incredibly beautiful, but also hurting, and it felt very natural for me to long to offer him something that would help with his healing. I had a token with an Angel of Healing on it that a dear friend had given me, and I felt divinely compelled to pass this angel on to him as a symbol of what my heart instinctively felt for him, even if this was not yet outwardly explored or expressed.

A couple of years later when I was living in Vancouver working on my master's degree in transpersonal psychology, he told me that he was interested in coming to visit me. He was in the process of ending a long-term relationship, felt emotional and vulnerable, and was drawn to see me and to explore the beauty of British Columbia. At that time, I was in an interesting space regarding intimate relationships, having just completed a three-month sabbatical from men in order to explore what unhealthy dynamics I was playing out in that realm. So I was welcoming, yet cautious. I didn't want to jump into anything, and yet there was a part of me that always wondered if he and I might have a certain romantic chemistry if we had the opportunity to be together again.

On April Fool's Day, 2006, he arrived in Vancouver. There were those eyes, that playfulness, and that heart. And as they say, the rest is history. Very soon we began dating, and since that time we have had our joys and challenges in good measure. But such is how love plays itself out in our perfectly imperfect human relationships. Our bond of deep friendship, love, and spiritual connection continually calls us to "step up" with one another instead of "stepping out" when things get tough. And trust me, they have gotten extremely tough. Twice I actually did step out, but the depth of love between us called me back. One of my deepest struggles with our relationship involves my fears about how we can be together on this earth when he co-owns and runs a retreat center in Costa Rica and I am an urban Canadian woman with connections, ambitions, and desires that run beyond an isolated valley in Central America. Where will we live? How can we work? What will be the balance of this life together? How can we afford it? Many unanswered questions swirl inside my worry-filled mind about our life, and in this fearful state of being, my heart knows no peace.

I have freaked out and tried to push him away many times so that I could perhaps attract a man with a life more in harmony with my own—a partner with a life that I can understand and somewhat control. However, on a deep level, I believe that this uncertain, "foolish" relationship has been exactly what I've needed in order to learn many of the love lessons I signed up for. And this precious man, this unique individual unlike any other I've known, perhaps he's precisely the one to capture my heart and soul in love in order to bring us both to the next step in our evolution. There have been many sobering moments when I've wondered if I am being courageous or downright crazy to continue nourishing this love. I usually end up accepting that it is probably a good mixture of the two. And in terms of the crazy part, I think it is good crazy. It's the kind of crazy that many rational people would say could never work. And it is the kind of crazy that many dreamers choose to believe in, sometimes against all odds.

The first time I stepped out of this relationship was in the fall of 2007. I had finished my master's degree the previous June, moved back to Toronto for the summer, and felt ready to set the world on fire with my passion for the healing arts. However, I found myself crying as I fell asleep at night and as I awakened in the morning for a few days before we left for Costa Rica at the end of August. I still had a vision of living my life back in my hometown, close to my family and heart-tribe of friends, launching my integrated healing practice, and thriving in every possible way. I felt this dream disintegrating with every step I took toward him and Costa Rica, yet I continued to take steps in his direction.

It was so hard for us both. He could sense my sadness, which discouraged him. How many women would *kill* for the chance to join him in paradise?! Why was I so resistant? I don't think he fully understood how vital my life in Toronto was and how much I felt I was giving up by being with him. That September, it was rainy, cool, and isolated at his retreat center in Costa Rica, and I felt deeply lonely, sad, and depressed. I was unable to enjoy the beauty of the place because if felt so far from almost everyone and everything I longed to be surrounded by. I was deeply torn in two very distinct pieces.

One afternoon as we were relaxing together, I asked him a very important question. "What do you really want for your life?" In that moment, the two main things I wanted to know were 1) where he wanted to live, and 2) if he ever wanted to get married. From love, I longed to know what was true for him and to honor what felt most true for me. He stated that he wanted to spend most of the year where he lived and worked in Costa Rica, and to travel to Canada, Italy, and other beautiful parts of the world during the slower months of his business. And, he never really wanted to get married.

When I took in his truth and weighed it with my own—which involved wanting to live most of my life in Toronto near my family and friends, to travel and be on retreat in beautiful parts of the world a minority of that time, and to be married—it seemed obvious that we were not in harmony with one another. And so, as painful as it was, I chose to leave. I felt I was doing the loving thing by letting go and allowing each of us the possibility of finding a new love with partners who were in sync with our desires. I never stopped loving him, but I couldn't go on living a life that felt wrong for me, which felt like a waste of so much beauty.

Months passed, and I built a new life for myself in Toronto. I tried dating a few men to move on. He kept reaching out to me from Costa Rica, trying desperately to re-unite—even promising to marry me and live in Toronto if that was what it would take. But I couldn't accept him betraying his truth to be with me, which would have been equally tragic and unsuccessful as my doing the same. Then one morning, I woke up in the bedroom of a man I had recently met. As I looked around, I knew that wasn't where I really wanted to be. Nothing felt right. Soon after that experience, I was in the grocery checkout line when I noticed a sweet two-year-old girl who looked exactly how I pictured me and my previous partner's child, if we were to have one. On some level, I wondered if we might still have children together as crazy and unlikely as that seemed in that moment.

Finally, one day in a hot yoga class, I set my intention to listen deep within my heart to what was true and to what I should do with my persistent love for this beautiful man. I stretched, sweated, and danced in and out of my analytical mind until the end of class when, in the deep relaxation of Savasana, I asked God from a clear and surrendered inner space what love would have me do in this particular moment and circumstance. If the divine directive was to let go, I could keep doing that. If it was to hold on and keep going, God willing, I could do that, too. I just needed to know. This time I got an answer that was clear, strong, and undeniable: *"Find a way."*

Love would have us find a way. I had my answer, and now

I needed to respond with action. My heart said "Yes," my head continued to ask "How?," and my spirit led me forward to rejoin him in a new vision of a life that includes Costa Rica and Canada, honours his truth and mine, and seeks balance in a way that feels good to us both. It is a fine balance that continues to challenge us deeply, even though we both have a big desire to allow it to work. I truly feel like our relationship has been a purifying fire in which we get the chance, through experience, to gain increasing clarity about who we are and the lives we long to lead in this world. I am ever aware of Kahlil Gibran's wisdom on the topic of love, how it enables us to reach our highest heights, and shakes us to our depths in our clinging to the earth.

Having stepped out and then back in again, we have come to trust that this love we share is not rational, logical, or controllable. It simply is. And now we are married after having taken the big leap into that sacred commitment. It feels wonderful to live the mystery and magic of love with him daily. No matter what form my love life takes over the years or how it evolves, I trust the journey of this Big Love, choosing time and again to live and love fully rather than cowering and accepting a half-life in fear. And even when fears come up and I feel totally shaken inside, I do my best to love myself right where I'm at. The soul speaks gently and persistently of love to us all, beckoning us to listen and respond. We always have that beautiful option.

One thing I know for certain: There is always great wisdom and beauty in love, and it always calls us to open our heart and wake up to the truth living inside each of us. Love enlivens us to have the courage to live that heavenly truth with our feet on the ground in this mucky, messy, beautiful earth. The highest soul love must integrate with the grounded earthly path in order to find its greatest fulfillment. I still feel like an amateur student in love training, with a multitude of lessons yet to be learned. Each love I've encountered, each wounding and healing of my heart, each tear and smile, have all led me to this present moment, which is perfect just as it is. I am love, and so are you. We must not allow despair to stop us from having the courage to live more and to love fully. There is a famous saying: "Love like you've never been hurt." Wise words. Beauty's Way beckons us above all else to love, for it is love that awakens beauty in all things—always and in all ways.

Beauty tips for love

1. What does your personal love story look like? Sound like? Feel like? Smell like? Write it. Paint it. Cook it. Sculpt it. Sing it. Walk it. Dance it. Drum it. Try new and creative ways to express your love-path and see how your love-life opens up.

2. How does love beckon you in your life right now? Is it a relationship that invites you to step up, be brave, and break down barriers long held in fear? Is it a career that brings you deeper into service for the greater good? Is love calling you to some sacred time of self-care and self-nurturing that allows you to expand in your love for yourself? Is it calling you to forgive someone who hurt you because they were afraid? Listen to love's call in this very moment and consider what your next step is in responding with an answer.

3. The song *Power of Love* by Frankie Goes to Hollywood gives excellent advice: "Make love your goal". Practice walking through your day repeating silently and consistently to yourself: "Love is my only goal." How does that affect your thoughts? Your actions? Your behaviours? Your choices? Your state of mind, heart, and being? Is there any greater goal than this, really? Journal or share with a friend what it was like to devote a whole twenty-four hours simply to *love*. And then try it again tomorrow.

Chapter 5

The Beauty of Friendship

"In the end we are all children, walking through this strange land between birth and death. None of us knows much. The best we can do is stay close and hold hands."
Katagiri Roshi

"Friendship doubles our joy and divides our grief."
Swedish Proverb

Heart-bonds

There is a specific kind of love that deserves a whole chapter of its own, a love so rich with beauty that it yearns to be expanded upon. It is a love without which this exposition would be incomplete, a love beyond the challenges of family and the comings and goings of intimate partners, even beyond the lessons to be learned from our enemies and teachers. It is the love that exists between true friends. I have been deeply blessed to have many kindred spirits on this life path from an early age up to the present, and I could write a whole chapter about each one of these precious souls who grace my life and comprise my heart-tribe. One particular, spectacular friendship has stood the test of time, as one woman more than lives up to the term "best friend."

I met Penny in the summer of 1989 at a Christian camp in the lake district of Ontario. From the moment I first saw her, I was enraptured. She was the epitome of a beautiful, healthy, vibrant, charismatic, intelligent, and sensitive young woman. At that time, I had been struggling with my health for many years, and meeting her was like finding a reflection of the young girl I could have been if I were well—the person I actually was in the essence of my being. We weren't part of the same clique at camp that week; however, there was an undeniable connection and draw between us, and I found myself in awe of this lovely girl. She was so full of life; she radiated such a bright light and inspired me deeply even though I hardly knew her. The night we returned to our respective homes, full of sentimental memories and still brimming with post-camp excitement, we enjoyed a great telephone chat and felt the first inklings of a blessed friendship that would become a rich godsend to us both for many, many years to come.

Although we lived in opposite ends of the city, attended different high schools, and had our own distinct circle of friends, we managed to stay in touch by phone and frequent visits. Through the years, we also had the chance to live with one another in Montreal, where we started McGill University together, and during subsequent summers in Muskoka. Penny became family to me, both because she was such a sweet, gracious, and consistent presence in my life, and because she was the one I lived with when my nuclear family fell apart at the seams. I have no idea what I would have done without her unconditional love, support, and endless patience as I went through various phases of pain and struggle on my path. She was always the figure in my life and in my dreams who led me through the dark times into the light—the one who made the big, overwhelming mountains transform into gentle valleys. And even more, she was amazing at simply sitting with me in the tough times, holding my hand, sharing the tremendous goodness and generosity in her heart.

Penny repeatedly brought light to my darkness just by being there for me and with me. I have learned so much from the rich wisdom that comes from such a beautiful way of solidly witnessing another human being through the inevitable ups and downs of life. We shared an abundance of wonderful times together, and so many memories pop up when I think about her. One night, early in our university experience, we shared a whole homemade blueberry pie, which was full of pleasure in the moment but left us (not surprisingly!) cramped up and quite sick later on. We both still agree, however, that it was well worth it. We were waitresses together at a restaurant in Muskoka, and we ended up hiding out one time in the kitchen freezer when we were "in the weeds," as they say in serving terms when you're so busy that you feel you'll never make it through. We were ready to quit right then and there with our tables filled and guests all waiting to be served. We laughed so hard and uncontrollably at a meditation gathering that we had to leave or get kicked out, so we left. And we used to get in my car on warm, summer nights, singing exuberantly along to Garth Brooks' melodies while we drove miles and miles simply to follow the sunset. I could fill a whole book with our memories, experiences and adventures. We all deserve such amazing times with a dear and kindred-spirit friend.

Purifying fires

Along with all the great memories of Penny's and my friendship are times that were challenging and rough— times that broke my heart and shook the foundation of my world because I loved Penny so much that I couldn't stomach being anything but great with her. Our rocky, powerful, and healing times prepared us for what we would eventually face in intimate relationships that were based on a strong bond of friendship. I recall one time in Muskoka when I was deeply troubled by the escalating pain and conflict within my family; my body and mind were so weak that I could hardly digest a thing. At that time, Penny was struggling too, trying to find her own way in that particular chapter of her life. It was thus not surprising that within the density of our mutual challenges, we occasionally gave in to the temptation to project our pain on to each other and were less than successful at holding space for one another in the way we were accustomed to.

I don't remember the exact details of our argument in the little cottage we were renting that summer on Moon River, but those are not the most important things to recall. What remains embedded in my memory is what I felt in the car as we were driving home one midsummer day when, out of a desire to comfort me in my pain, Penny gently touched my leg, letting me know I was not alone, that she was with me. At the first sensation of her gentle touch, my body became rigid and I felt myself close up and shake inside; there was no way I could receive or withstand her pure extension of love. I pushed her away promptly and coldly. As sad as it was, I just couldn't let her love in. I was too angry, scared, and frustrated to be open and receptive. I didn't want to hurt her by refusing her kindness, but I felt like I had no control over myself or my reaction. After an extremely long and painful silence, which in real time lasted maybe fifteen minutes, we arrived home and were able to honestly and vulnerably face each other, courageously taking turns sharing our feelings, fears, and desires.

We both knew that we had to clear this tension or it would break us, and neither of us needed any further wounding. That one exchange, across the kitchen table, full of raw honesty and many deep-hearted tears, taught me much about what it means to become vulnerable and accountable; it also illustrated the power of choosing to join with someone you love instead of furthering the experience of separation and division. It took every bit of energy I had to really hear her, cultivating loving neutrality when she shared what was being triggered inside her that had nothing to do with me. Then I was challenged to stay receptively and non-reactively open when what she had to say felt hurtful because it *did* relate to me, which involved Penny's concerns about my recent behaviour. Much of what she shared rubbed against a tender wound within me, and I had to do my best to remember that she was not making me bad or wrong, but was merely sharing her experience of being with me in the midst of my messy pain. In the end, Penny heard me, with a loving ear and a compassionate heart, and I slowly began to feel safe again in this bond between us that I was learning could withstand so much more than just fun times. It was tough, purifying, and ultimately beautiful. Our friendship is richer and deeper for being able to go through the hard times and come out strengthened rather than broken.

Angel-friend

I will remember vividly another incredibly powerful experience I had with Penny for the rest of my life. In that instance, her love-in-action helped me to not give up or give in when things were rougher than rough, lower than low, more desperate than I could have ever imagined. I had been visiting Penny and her sister, Samantha, in Montreal for a weekend. I enviously witnessed the full and rich university life they were enjoying—the life I had left behind years earlier to pursue other dreams and adventures. In that moment, I reflected painfully on my currently bleak situation: I was living back at my mother's house, feeling trapped both economically and emotionally, while at the same time struggling with an eating disorder that I was just beginning to face head-on, an illness based in great fear that had reached new heights—or rather, lows.

Looking back, I see that what happened the night before I left Montreal became a turning point in my healing journey. I went to bed early and had a terrifying nightmare. In the dream, I was lying on the ground and a man drove over me with his car, severing my head from my body. Somehow, I had managed to set my head back where it belonged, but the connection remained very weak and fragile. Then he picked me up and started throwing me in the air like a rag doll, and once again my head fell off its perch; I was left broken in two and feeling completely disconnected. I woke up in a feverish sweat and went to the bathroom with a dry throat, a pounding heart, an aching stomach, and an overall feeling of weakness that left me dizzy and disoriented. I was experiencing a full-blown panic attack, and I had no idea what to do with myself. I feared that I might die right then and there.

Sitting on the toilet, feeling completely lost, I rested my feet on tiptoe because it felt too painful to be in this body, on this earth, both feet fully on the ground. I called for Penny to come and be with me, because I was afraid. I began to feel my consciousness leaving my body and heading diagonally toward the top right-hand corner of the bathroom. I recognise this experience in hindsight as a highly conscious experience of dissociation—a sense of leaving my body because it no longer felt safe inside. Penny was my angel, once again. She sat with me, held my hands, and breathed with me, which helped to bring me back down to earth and feel somewhat okay again. Her presence soothed me long enough to enable me to gather my strength, set my two feet flat on the ground again, get some sleep, and then make my way back to Toronto. I was boldly ready to face my life as it was, step by step.

As I drove home, I knew that I was awakening to what was really not working in my life; I felt chillingly aware of some changes I needed to make, and quickly. The fear inside me started to overpower my best intentions, and after driving for almost an hour I felt myself losing my breath and drowning in anxiety. I was in yet another horrible panic attack. I tried my best to breathe and calm myself, but to no avail. I was in no shape to drive. Like it or not, I was going to have to ask for help.

Pulling over at the nearest pit-stop along the side of the highway, I first called Penny. Samantha answered and was sweet, gentle, and kind with me. She wisely suggested that I ask someone working there to help me because she and Penny didn't have access to a car, and they were both deep in the heart of exam time. She promised she would let Penny know what was happening. It was then that I realized I might have to go to the hospital here, in the middle of nowhere, which didn't do anything good for my anxiety level. What would I do with the car? Who would come and get me? How would I get through this? Why was this happening to me?

There were many things I did not know in that moment, but

the one thing I knew for sure was that I needed help, and I needed it immediately. I gathered every ounce of courage and humility I could muster and went to the counter at the coffee shop, asking the woman attendant if she could help me. I was crying and must have looked like a royal mess. By the sheer grace of God, she was a wonderful, compassionate human being who took me to the side and talked to me until the ambulance arrived. The next hour or two is a bit of a foggy blur in my memory, but I do remember arriving to the hospital and being seen fairly quickly by an intern who checked my vital signs and pronounced me in decent enough health to be released if someone could pick me up.

My first instinct was to call my mother and ask her and her boyfriend to come and get me, which would allow one of them to drive home the car I had left behind. My mom seemed concerned about me, but she had a class to teach that night that she felt she couldn't miss. She didn't think she could come and get me until the following day, but she wasn't even sure if that would work. I would have to find another way. I sat in that white, cold hospital room and prayed the most raw, sincere prayer for help. Within moments, I miraculously felt a rush of God's love and tenderness wash over me. I felt a new sense of faith and strength sweep in from God-Knew-Where, and I had the first calm thought that somehow it was all going to be okay. I was going to get well again, and I would be a Woman Who Ran with the Wolves (based on one of my favourite books by Clarissa Pinkola Estes) instead of a Woman Who Crawled on the Floor with the Insects. I still didn't know how on earth I was going to get out of that hospital, but somehow I would move forward from this embarrassing and painful place.

I got up out of the bed and went into the hall to make another phone call. It was then I saw the one person I was happiest to see walking toward me with a big smile of love on her face: Penny. I had no idea how she got there or what we were going to do, but I remember how absolutely thankful I was to have a friend like this who would do *whatever it took* to be there for me in my hour of real need. She was a true angel of light in a very shadowy and scary

71

time, and I will never forget what she did to help me get out of that place and begin a new chapter of healing in my life. She had found out which hospital I was in and called her professor whose exam she was going to have to miss, told him there was a family emergency, and requested a re-write for the test. She then rented a car without thought of what we were going to do with it and came to me. Plain and simple, she did everything she could so that I didn't have to go through such a painful time all alone. Such is the beauty of radical love. God bless that woman!

Giving and receiving

Life is always seeking balance, and where there is giving there will also always be a chance to receive. Several years later, it came to be my time to act with generous, loving friendship for Penny in her time of need. I got an e-mail early one morning at 6:00 a.m. with the following subject heading: "Early labour at St. Mike's." I thought maybe Penny was forwarding me a story or a joke, because she was not due to give birth to her second child until early February; this being mid-December, it was much too early for the e-mail to be referring to *her*. But this was no joke or story; it was a very personal e-mail stating that she had indeed gone into early labour at approximately midnight the night before. She asked me to please send some Reiki healing energy to her and the baby, and to come by if I could to St. Michael's hospital sometime that day. I went downstairs to my morning meditation and yoga space, lit a candle, and began to pray and send healing thoughts and energies to them. Immediately, I was struck with the instinct to get my butt off the yoga mat and onto the subway to *be with her* right in that moment when she needed *me* the most.

When Penny's first child was born in Toronto, I was at school in Vancouver and thus unable to be present with her at that critical and poignant time. Now here I was just a few miles away instead of in Costa Rica, where I would be in two days. I could go to her! And so I did. I gladly went into unconditional and unlimited loving service to this woman who is my dearest friend and whose life I cherish, which often brings me to tears. It was wonderful to care for her and be present to her in a way that only true friends can. Fortunately, as she rested and relaxed, the baby growing in her womb also calmed down. The labour halted for a little while, giving the baby more time to grow and develop in the warmth and comfort of her belly before entering into the world. Penny and I both felt incredibly blessed to have that experience together, to once again nurture our connection with the ongoing dance of giving and receiving, which is the lifeblood of any bond of all beautiful friendships everywhere.

In January of 2009, Barack Obama was inaugurated as the forty-fourth president of the United States of America. Whether you like the "Yes, We Can!" man or not, whether you agree or disagree with his politics, it is undeniable that his presence, not just in his own country but in the whole world, speaks volumes about the evolving state of consciousness on the planet. The night Obama won the election, television stations were broadcasting celebrations from all over the globe—from Africa to Australia to Israel and beyond. It felt like the Super Bowl of politics, with hope as the victor. In his inaugural speech, President Obama spoke many inspiring words, offering in that relatively short address to the public his overarching commitments and intentions as president of the United States.

One comment he made stands out for me, and I believe it spoke to many people's hearts on a global scale. He offered his hand in friendship and willingness to dialogue with any nation that extended its hand in return. This was an amazing opportunity for miracles to happen, for fear to be overcome by love, for peace to take the place of war. Nations must make friends with one another if we are to thrive as a planet rather than self-destruct.

The same is true on a smaller scale. Therefore, all that we do to extend a benevolent hand in friendship in this world adds to the smile of love that symbolizes a world at peace with itself. And to be part of creating that world, my dear friends, is an incredibly beautiful and powerful opportunity. Extend your open hand to the extended hand of benevolence and allow the joint energy of friendship to change your life and transform our society and our world. Beauty is born of such sacred unions and communions.

Beauty tips for friendship

1. Who was your first friend? What do you remember most about them? Are you still in touch? What does this person represent for you now, if anything?

2. A wise teacher of mine often stated that only what we are not giving is what is lacking in any situation. If you are having trouble with a friend and feeling like your needs aren't being met, how might you *give* what it is you would like to receive from them? What happens when you do this? Notice.

3. Who is your best or closest friend now? What is it that you share together that stands out so powerfully? Have you shared with that person recently how much they mean to you? If one of you were to leave this earth tomorrow, what might remain unspoken? Lovingly dare to communicate that sentiment today.

4. What do you value most in friendship? And what do you feel are the greatest gifts you offer your friends? Have a party or celebration to honor your friendships. When all else fails, the true love of friends remains. *Celebrate that!*

5. Is there a friend whom you have lost touch with who is very dear to your heart? What stops you from reaching out to them? Is there some reconciliation to be done? Can you take the first steps? Cultivate beauty in that friendship—step *fully* into doing your part and give space for miracles to happen.

Chapter 6

The Beauty of Freedom

"Then you shall know the truth,
And the Truth shall set you free."
Jesus Christ

"I don't know if I am free, but I feel a lot of freedom."
Robert Wolanski

The attraction to freedom

Defining freedom is as elusive as trying to define love. Freedom is a state of being, an emotion, a practice, a gift, a goal, and a dream ever longing to be realized. What is it about freedom that lures us out of our various forms of imprisonment and promises to make our hearts sing and our souls smile? Whatever it is, when we taste it, our bodies are filled with vital enthusiasm, our minds are cleansed and sobered, and life feels good simply in the living of it. I have an inkling that freedom is so sweet because it is the birthright of every living being. I believe we are born free—authentically who we are without any traces of conditioning just yet. And it is through the course of our lives that we are bound to find out what it means to lose our freedom to the demands of family, community, and society, to our fear-based egos falsely thinking they need to protect us from anything and everything, to whatever causes us to deviate from being true to ourselves. The healing journey is awakened when we open to the process of piecing together the parts of ourselves we disconnected from, denied, and split off for one reason or another. As we gather ourselves into wholeness, we can taste that sweet freedom once again.

The dream of freedom

I had a powerful dream a few years ago that felt distinctly like Divine wisdom filtering through my psyche while I slept. At that time, I was working as a receptionist at The Yoga Studio in Toronto, and was dreaming of the life I might live if I fully followed my aspirations and began to manifest in the material world the potential I knew lay within me like a buried treasure waiting to be discovered, opened, shared. Even though I had a strong, palpable sense of the greater life that could emerge if I courageously brought forward the life inside me, at that time I felt stuck—stone-cold stuck between some very hard walls and bound by strong chains. I was only working part-time due to the remaining health challenges resulting from CFS, earning little more than minimum wage, and living in my mother's basement apartment with no clear idea of how or when I would begin to step forward into a more fulfilled and empowered existence. But I wanted it—*badly.*

Then came the dream. In it, I was heading to work one morning at The Yoga Studio, and even though I knew the way to get there like the back of my hand, I kept getting lost on the subway system. Instead of arriving at my stop, I somehow found myself walking into an Anthony Robbins motivational conference. He was on stage, speaking to the crowd with his energetic personality and famous charisma. I heard him say he was going to invite three members of the audience up to the stage so that he could personally help them realize one of their dreams. He wanted to awaken the giant in them. They just had to claim it and be willing to take the necessary steps. To my absolute shock and delightful surprise, especially since I wasn't really supposed to be part of the conference, my name was called.

I eagerly took my place on stage, and when Anthony asked me what I truly wanted for my life, I told him I wanted to write and publish a book. I even shared with him my vision for what the book would entail, and he asked if I was sincerely committed to making my dream come true. Immediately, "Yes!" burst from my whole being out through my mouth. Then I realized how late I was for work. I left the conference, making my way to the studio. This time I found it without a problem and was filled with excitement, passion, and purpose. When I arrived at work, no one even noticed that I was late. I started preparing one of the studios for the day, and as I swept the floor and dusted the windowsills, I noticed a gorgeous golden journal sitting on the ledge. I was magnetically drawn to it. As I picked it up, I saw the front cover filled with hands of spiraling light. Inside was a beautiful and powerful inscription:

"We are Daughters of the Goddess

Freeing ourselves with ink."

Amazing. Through the power of the dream, I found myself reconnecting with my freedom path. I continue to fulfill this destiny as I write each word on every page of all the books I create and take the steps necessary to make real my dreams.

Free to be

We all have an important story to tell, and if we really listened to one another, we would find that even though the specific details may vary, the overarching themes of love, loss, and longing touch us all. I attended a Feminine Spirituality conference in Victoria, British Columbia., in my early twenties, and was deeply inspired to see women, men, and children of all ages, cultures, and religious traditions gathering together to share stories, insights, rituals, wisdom, and love. It was a safe and celebratory environment in which to explore healing from the divine feminine perspective. The most memorable workshop session was led by an older Buddhist woman who had obviously witnessed and experienced many things, both wonderful and challenging, in her rich, full life. I sat in one of the back rows of the auditorium, yet my heart was awake, front and center. I listened intently to her words of sheer grace and practical wisdom. Her greatest offering to us was a formula she had learned and used for many years, which assisted her in finding her own personal sense of freedom, and a guideline that she gave to the oppressed, suppressed, and compressed everywhere. It went like this:

"Think what you think.
Feel what you feel.
Know what you know."

In other words, be yourself in all ways, just as you are, without pretense or justification. Even if others might deem you wrong or judge you for the way that you are, take no heed. Be boldly, courageously, and radically *you*.

I am free

Since embracing my own healing journey, I have been acting as a midwife for birthing others' freedom. In the process, I keep peeling away more layers of my own personal imprisonment. Within twenty-four hours of my choosing to muster up my courage and listen to my heart's voice yet again, trust its leadings, and head back to Costa Rica to give things another chance with my partner, I got a fate-filled e-mail from my dear friend, Iwona, who lives in Warsaw. She owned the beautiful yoga studio I worked at in Vancouver, and she was now living and working in her homeland of Poland, full steam ahead in the corporate world. She told me that she was stressed to the max, beginning to feel that stress affecting her health, and that she needed help.

Iwona wanted to come to wherever I was and spend two to three weeks doing some intensive healing work, including yoga, Reiki, massage—anything and everything I could do to help her come back to her center, her sense of wellness, and ultimately, her soul. Of course, my first instinct was to tell her to come to the magical, mystical retreat center in Costa Rica where I was soon headed. It all felt divine. Perfect. I had shivers all through my being, the kind of shivers you get when you feel and really know that a Greater Force is at work in the direction of much goodness. So it was settled. She would meet me in Costa Rica where we would spend three luscious weeks together, my full attention on facilitating and holding space for whatever she might need at this point in her healing.

The first week was taken up with her simply arriving and transitioning from the cold, gray winter of Warsaw life to the sunny, warm, tropical, and wild weather of a Costa Rica summer. It took a few days for Iwona to carry out some important communications back and forth with her colleagues in Poland, but once the big project she had been working on was complete, she was able to relax more deeply into simply being where she was, allowing herself the pleasure of dropping into the experience of the present. Little by little, she began to notice things that she had been oblivious to just the day before, from little items such as a wrought-iron angel in the restaurant holding a beautiful amethyst crystal to big natural structures like the volcano right in front of us. Iwona was amazed at how her senses began to open up as she viewed her external environment and also as she began to attune to her inner world. There was daily yoga, massage, Reiki, long walks talking about life, and later, some time at the ocean followed by adventures to hot springs and to a rustic ranch where we enjoyed horseback riding and hiking to a blue waterfall.

It is always so interesting to notice the way things work out in life, usually not as we plan them. The universe seems to take our strategies and blueprints and add its own creative twists and playful turns, and we end up with something different from what we had expected, but divine in its own way nonetheless. At the last minute, just before I left Toronto to catch my flight to Costa Rica, I rummaged through some old CDs to see if there was anything that might be helpful for Iwona. I found "Grace" by Snatam Kaur, a Kundalini angel-woman whose songs and chants are a true taste of heaven on earth. Knowing Iwona's rich and meaningful connection to the Kundalini tradition, I brought the CD with me. With a five-hour layover in Houston, I had plenty of time to sit and pray and to continue creating a plan for her three-week healing adventure. As I sat at my designated gate, laptop on lap, I compiled a list of various chants and prayers that have been powerful gifts in my life at critical moment of transformation, thinking I would offer these to her as well.

As it turned out, one particular track on the "Grace" CD, rather than my carefully planned agenda, was the crown jewel of her experience that helped bring Iwona back to herself, her connection to God, her soul, her inner freedom, her bliss. The chant is called "Ra Ma Da Sa." Even though she had worked with it before, something in the hours of its repetition, as she sat in meditation in the healing tree house with her arms and heart wide open to receive the grace of God, brought her out of the wild and manic ruminations of the mind and back into the vast realm of the awakening heart. Her deep and undisturbed sense of peace was silently and patiently waiting to meet her again. The taste of this chant was so delectable to her being that she could do nothing but share her joy with everyone willing to receive it.

It was such a beautiful transformation to witness, and her claiming of freedom was contagious. Iwona had many revelations of new paths opening up in her life. Choices had to be made, priorities had to be set, yet what was most vital was this connection to God, to the universe, to infinite love, to her own breath, voice, and spirit which was the very source and sustenance of her freedom. She even changed her name, adding three very appropriate middle names, so that she became "Iwona I Am Free Kozak." We are all entitled to adopt those three middle names as we are all entitled to freedom, however that may look, feel, smell and taste to us. It is up to each one of us to remember it, claim it, and live it. That takes great courage and brings tremendous, grounded joy.

Not long after Iwona's personal freedom breakthrough, she decided to lead a retreat with the theme "I Am Free" for her friends, family, and yoga students from Poland. For two weeks, this lovely group of individuals joined together at our retreat center in Costa

Rica to go deep in meditation and kundalini yoga, to enjoy the beauty and magic of this country, and to explore what freedom truly meant to each one of them. I offered bodywork and energy work sessions in our tree-top healing room, and witnessed amazing openings, releases, and transformations within each participant. One man in particular inspired the second quotation at the beginning of this chapter. Robert had just come to the end of a very powerful Reiki session when he slowly opened his eyes, gazed tenderly at me, and spoke the following words, "I don't know if I am free, but I feel a lot of freedom." Freedom offers us many tastes of her sweetness and glimpses of her vastness on this beautiful life journey.

Freedom's divine structure

One particular lesson stuck with me through the years and transformed my understanding of freedom. While studying Eastern Religions in university, I was still very young, naïve, and idealistic, as one in her early twenties tends to be without the wisdom of experience and the ripeness of maturity. Freedom, in my view, was the ability to do anything you want with no limits, restrictions, or boundaries. I had the image of a bird flying free and experienced only brief peak moments that allowed me to sense what that could feel like in the human realm. Freedom always seemed to come from spirit. My Zen Buddhist monk teacher helped bring my ideas of freedom back down to earth when he shared a powerful lesson about freedom, which included anatomy and physiology as its base.

The teaching focused on the arm and the elbow, and the ability to have freedom of movement. Without the intricate structure of tissues, muscles, ligaments, and tendons, there would be no ability to move. If such a structure were not in place, brilliantly designed and working in harmony, the arm would hang loose and have no ability to move through space, to facilitate the hand picking up objects, or to caress the skin of another. The structure itself—including boundaries, limits, and conditions—is actually the reason that freedom is possible. I had thought it was the exact opposite. In this human realm, we work best within the structures and systems that are in place. We have the choice to oppose those that suppress us and to celebrate those that nourish us, all the while living the fascinating journey of attempting to discern one from the other.

We can fly because we have wings made of hope and faith that can soar to heights and forever keep dreaming. We have feet that ground us to the earth, reminding us to be humble and to walk mindfully on our unique life path. And we have tender, awakening hearts that with every pulse urge us to dare to love and be loved with greater and greater capacity. Freedom is always awake, alive, and beautiful in our midst.

Beauty tips for freedom

1. When in your life have you felt most trapped/stuck/blocked/not free? Lovingly and compassionately explore the circumstances of your life at that time: your belief system, what you were giving power to, the thoughts that were dominating your mind space, the emotions that were moving inside you.

2. When have you felt most free? Same deal: what was going on in your life, your heart, your mind, your body, and your spirit at that time?

3. If you were to take a step in the direction of your greatest freedom, what would it be? What holds you back from doing so? What could inspire you to take that step?

4. If you truly knew and believed that your freedom was not dependent on anything outside yourself, what would your inner voice tell you right now about your relationship to freedom? How free are you on a scale of zero to ten (ten being the most free)? What would it take for you to move up the scale? Acceptance? Forgiveness? Self-love and care? Healthy boundaries? Give yourself permission to claim what you need to be free.

5. If you accept the maxim that the truth sets you free, what truth do you personally need to acknowledge and give space for in order to live in a more liberated way? Begin each sentence: "The truth is…" and finish it on paper, over and over again, noticing what comes up. A word of loving caution: This exercise could be highly illuminating and may change the course of your life forever.

Part III:

Honouring the Beauty of the West

——◦✤✤◦——

We turn our awakening hearts to the West and we give great thanks for:
Times of deep letting go
Harvest of plenty
Sweet surrender into what is
Nature's brilliant display of colourful ecstasy
The warm, rich, comforting taste of home
Cooler days, cooler nights, freshness in the air
The beginnings of turning inward
Autumn colors and flavours
Crackling leaves and the smoky smell of bonfires
Giving thanks
Thinning veils between the worlds
Falling into fall
Falling in love
Just falling….
HO!

Chapter 7

The Beauty of Pain

"Pain is God's megaphone to a deaf world."
C.S. Lewis

"Your pain is the breaking of the shell that encloses your understanding."
Kahlil Gibran

The voice of pain

I have always felt a strong resonance with that first quote by C.S. Lewis, because I believe with the entirety of my being that pain carries vital information, divine messages that are calling us to healing rather than bearing down on us in meaningless punishment. Often the voice of Spirit whispers gently and lovingly in our ear, wanting to assist us in finding balance, harmony, and our way in this world. When we are out of sync, when we are discordant, when we are going down a path that doesn't speak to our highest good or the intentions we truly desire to put "out there" from the center of our being, these whispers come.

Often we are so busy with the many demands and activities of our everyday lives that we don't heed the warning signs. Or we hear the whispers and are aware of their wisdom, yet lack the courage to follow the lead of this holy voice. In the name of truth, we must be still not only to know who our God is, but to hear her voice and follow her guidance. These whispers tend to grow louder over time, but often we remain unwilling to listen and heed the calls because to do so would mean changing things about our lives that might seem uncomfortable, senseless, or crazy to those around us.

And so, by divine grace, which can often seem more like holy nuisance, these soft and tender whispers grow into loud, shrill, ear-piercing screams as life tries desperately to get our attention. I offer you a personal example. I was once in a relationship with a man that had lasted almost three months. We were in the phase of beginning to learn about one another beyond sparking hormones and the compelling, mysterious power of attraction. We had a talk one day during which this man said that he didn't think he ever wanted to get married, and that although he was committed to monogamy for now, he would let me know if and when that ever changed. He claimed quite righteously that he desired a spiritually open relationship, yet what he really meant was that he didn't want to commit to anything and wanted to retain the freedom to stay open to new possibilities and possibly better options. Yuck. Almost immediately, both of my ears began to hurt with a ringing, tingling, and throbbing pain.

I didn't want to listen to what the pain had to say in that moment, because I didn't want to end the relationship just yet. Then came my inner dialogue: *Maybe what he said wasn't really true.* Perhaps what I wanted would somehow transform into something that he would come into harmony with over time. I didn't have to hear this or deal with it right away. And yet, day after day, the pain remained and grew stronger. I went to the doctor, hoping to find out that it was some bizarre ear infection that I could take something for and it would go away. No such luck. There was no medical explanation for what I was feeling. And yet whatever was going on was certainly having physiological ramifications, big time!

Finally, after two long weeks of agony, enough was enough. I woke up one Sunday morning and prayed the most sincere prayer to God that I could possibly utter in that moment. The prayer went like this: "Holy Beautiful Spirit of God, I am willing to hear. Whatever it is, I am willing to hear." This was my rhythmical mantra that rode the wave of nearly each and every breath: "I am willing to hear." Being an adept student of mind-body medicine, I had come to the analytical conclusion that this pain in my ear had to do with my blocking out what my partner was saying.

Once I let go of what I thought was right in order to make space for whatever was true, I humbly realized that I might have been mistaken. I remained calm, allowing a more neutral stance to wash over my mind and body, and became receptive and willing to agree with whatever the universe had to offer in terms of wisdom and guidance. What I realized in an illuminated, revelatory way was that it was *my* inner voice I was blocking out, and that was the source of my pain. I didn't want to hear my voice telling me that this was not a healthy relationship for me, that I did indeed want to get married one day to a man who wanted the same, and that the commitment of monogamy was something sacred to me.

It was in not hearing my own voice that I had blocked the flow of energy in my body, and this materialized in a nasty earache that didn't subside until I committed wholeheartedly to courageously and boldly honor my truth. This approach proved successful. I found myself that very afternoon speaking from my heart with this partner, telling him my feelings, and thereby ending the relationship. Almost immediately, the pain was gone. It was an incredible experience. I did have one brief relapse when he called to insist that he cared deeply for me, didn't want to lose me, and was willing to do anything to make it work. I was tempted to step back in; in that moment of weakness, the pain returned with a vengeance, so I couldn't do it. A part of me wished I wasn't so sensitive so that I could do whatever I wanted without my body rebelling whenever I was out of integrity. The other part of me, the best part of me, was incredibly thankful that my body speaks to me in all ranges of volume and tones and never gives up on me, even when I'm not listening.

Conscious pain

Over the course of my life, I have suffered from migraines when there is a high-pressure atmospheric system in my immediate environment, when I eat something with MSG, when I hold on to anger or resentment, when I don't get enough sleep, or when my hormones go into chaos mode just before the onset of my menstrual cycle. While working on this chapter, I got a horrific headache when I was thrown violently by a huge wave in the Pacific Ocean of Montezuma, Costa Rica, and my cervical vertebrae went completely out of alignment.

As I sat with the pain, breathed through it, and asked it if there is anything I could do to help release it, the message I got was straightforward and simple: Slow down. Rest. Don't worry. Ah, so that's it? Even though in that moment all was well, my worries about the future—its uncertainty and ambiguity—felt heavy, dark, and somber. Shortly after, I got into a minor car accident as I was pondering the pain and the worries. I took this is a big wake-up call, one on which I was not going to press the snooze button. I've learned that as I listen within and take the action healing calls for, I can create a new vibrational frequency of trust and presence. The pain subsides and I am left with a greater feeling of ease. It's a beautiful thing.

Pain and suffering

I am finding that messages about pain abound. I learned a new lesson about pain and suffering while attending a powerful meeting led by Dr. Alastair Cunningham, founder of the Healing Journey, a course for people living with and healing from cancer. It is a spiritually oriented group in which the principles of *A Course in Miracles* (a psycho-spiritual text and workbook) are explored in depth, especially as they relate to healing of mind and body as well as philosophies about sickness and health. We were talking openly that day about pain and suffering, dynamics highly familiar to those in the room.

One of the women eagerly shared a bit of information and an "aha" moment that changed her way of dealing with her struggles.

She said she learned from a meditation leader in Toronto, Philip Starkman, that pain multiplied by resistance equals suffering (P x R = S). Therefore, no matter how high the pain measured on your personal Richter scale, if the resistance is nil then the suffering is equally nil. Interesting. This thought must come from the same source as the saying "Pain is inevitable, suffering is optional," or "What you resist, persists." In other words, whenever we resist anything in life, we suffer. Acceptance is ultimately and always the shortest and most direct path toward peace and happiness—and acceptance is a daily spiritual practice.

Pain's deeper mysteries

A particularly intense experience with pain brought me to my knees (or to be accurate, into full fetal position) and taught me a great deal. It was the first day of my menstrual cycle. I was feeling okay although the onset of my period can sometimes signal a morning of intense abdominal cramping, intermittent fever, weakness, and the palpable feeling that I am having contractions. I went to work and began a ninety-minute healing session of massage and Reiki with my dear friend and Reiki student, Iwona.

I was half an hour into this treatment when I began to feel heat coursing through my body and my mouth became uncomfortably dry. The room felt like it was becoming smaller and smaller, and I found myself in a great deal of pain that refused to be silenced. I excused myself for a moment to go to the bathroom and attempted to regain my composure as "healer," but it was not in the cards. I re-entered the healing room and let Iwona know what was happening to me. She immediately insisted upon getting dressed and switching places so that she could shower me with Reiki in the midst of my struggle. Thank God for the angels we are blessed with in our lives! I had no choice but to release any sense of personal pride in terms of what *should* have been and gladly lay on the table ready to become the one being supported and nurtured.

The next hour consisted of waves of intense pain that felt like the most powerful contractions yet. I gained an illuminating realisation during that experience that pain carries an amazing potential to be a powerful portal into greater awareness and deep, to-the-core healing. Some may think that what I am about to share next is ludicrous and self-delusional; however, I have my faith about the reality of certain things that we have no way of explaining or understanding from our limited sense of what is possible in this life and beyond.

The previous year, I had a phone session with a woman healer who does Soul Essence work. She connects with your guides and angels and helps you to energetically clear old karmic residue from past lives that may be hindering your development in present life circumstances. At least that is how I understand it. In my session, this woman relayed to me a story from a past life in which I was pregnant and nearing delivery time. I was living in the desert and decided to travel to a different part of the land in order to begin a new and healthier life for myself and my baby. While on the path, alone and in the fullness of pregnancy, I went into labour, and in that feverish dance of consciousness merging with unconsciousness, I birthed my own child. There were complications of some type in the birthing, and my baby died in my arms. While the healer went through each detail of this story, I cried and released so many tears as I felt this ancient grief reawakening in me. I had to bury my baby there in the hot desert and continue on my way if I were to have a chance to live on. Nearing the edge of the new land and new life, I lost my strength and also passed away, alone. How devastatingly painful.

And so, in these times of menstrual agony, I have found myself feeling like I am systematically releasing karmic debris from that past life—sensations and emotions that have remained on some cellular level, waiting for me to be strong enough to feel, release, and somehow integrate the lessons from that life into the life I now lead. On that massage table, held in the healing hands, heart, and grace of my dear soul sister Iwona, I found myself symbolically giving birth, grieving, and letting go on a level deeper than ever before. I gained a new understanding of my great fear of becoming pregnant and delivering a child, my long-standing anxiety about being alone and unloved, and ultimately, my fear of death itself.

I faced all of this with a great deal of conscious compassion, shaking, shivering, and moaning on that table as I hugged my knees tightly against my chest, waiting until the cramping passed before getting up and moving on with my day. The remaining hours were fully devoted to extreme self-care. I was left weak and yet awakened by a new clarity and sense of awe in the face of how divine life is: it brings the healing you need, when you need it, when you're ready for it, and when your whole being can no longer hold on to that which is stifling the possibility for something new.

Because I did not resist my pain, it did not carry the usual quotient of suffering, and yet the experience was deeply transformative as I surrendered to it and witnessed its flow, rhythm, texture, and shape-shifting. As long as I didn't need the present moment to be anything other than what it was and as long as I didn't sabotage the process, I felt myself to be enveloped in an incredible feeling of love, peace, and trust that ran as deep and vast as anything I had ever known. There were slight flashes of resistance within me when the pain got so great I didn't think my physical body had the ability to endure any more. However, as I breathed through it and let go of the need to explain or numb it away, I remained a neutral and accepting witness to what was moving through me at a pace and scale that was far beyond my authority to control in any way. And what a gift that was.

Does pain always carry some sort of greater message and healing force? Or is it sometimes *just* pain? I don't pretend to know the definitive answer to that question. However, I do know that when I dialogue with my pain it is rare to find that it does *not* hold a message steering me in the direction of greater vitality and empowerment. Even if the message is simply to slow down, be gentle with myself, and to practice compassion, pain awakens, teaches, and reminds me that I am part of a vast collective human body experiencing a multitude of sensations from pain to pleasure, including all that falls beyond and between those two primal life dynamics.

Paul Ferrini's book *Love Without Conditions* reminds us that pain is the great equalizer in life, it is something all humans can relate to and exhibit compassion for in oneself and others. The same could be said about a great many things, but pain seems to bring us to our knees and dissolve away the fears and walls of the ego in a way nothing else can—that is, if we have the grace, wisdom, and courage to allow it. The hidden beauty of pain lies in its heightened capacity to liberate us from old ways of thinking and being and to move us into more expansive levels of consciousness and acceptance for the precious and exquisite beauty of our lives here on earth—just as they are.

Beauty tips for pain

1. Are you currently experiencing any pain in your life, be it physical, mental, emotional, or spiritual? Identify it: Give it a name and honour its presence as a holy messenger to you. Now take some deep breaths and notice where in your body, in this moment, the pain is living. Breathe right into that place and become as aware as possible, with all of your human senses, of the qualities of that pain. What color is it? Does it have texture? What temperature is it? If it were an animal, what would it be?

2. Take a moment now that you are really tuned in to your pain, and in that meditative space begin a dialogue with it. You might ask that pain what it is doing inside you, and what its message is for you. Does it speak with words or simply primal sounds? Listen. Does it want your attention? What does it want to say? Ask if there is anything you can do for it. Listen. First, listen. If it is challenging for you to tap into the pain in this way, you can also write yourself a letter from your pain, free-flow, and see what comes out. (Example: Begin with the words "Dear (insert your name)," followed by the message that comes through, uncensored and in stream-of-consciousness style, and complete the letter with "Love, Pain.")

3. Next is the time to respond. If you got some answers from your pain along with some guidance as to the next steps to honour yourself and transform the pain into something new, do your best to follow its instructions to the letter. Often we tend to stay in pain because it is serving some other purpose; it provides some pay-off; it is keeping us small and safe (not really, though) and protecting us (again, not really!) from taking

full responsibility for our lives. Are you sufficiently courageous and willing to move beyond your pain and into your joy? Or, if required, can you continue to sit compassionately with your pain until it is ready to shift? Be loving and gentle with yourself in this process, just like you would be with an innocent child who is suffering and needs soothing. There is no right or wrong way to do it, and the answers can only come from deep inside of *you*. Cultivate a new relationship to your pain and be transformed.

Chapter 8

The Beauty of Fear

"There is no fear in love; but perfect love casts out fear, because fear involves punishment, and the one who fears is not perfected in love."
1 John 4:18

"There are no guarantees. From the viewpoint of fear, none are strong enough. From the viewpoint of love, none are necessary."
Emmanuel Teney

"To fear love is to fear life, and those who fear life are already three parts dead."
Bertrand Russell

Dissecting fear

How on earth can one find beauty in fear? How can fear serve any purpose other than to thwart our most magnificent efforts toward a peaceful, powerful, and harmonious life? Of course, fear is a basic survival mechanism that can be critical when there is truly a need to fight, fly, or even freeze in defence of our lives. And yet, how often in our modern world is that truly the case? How many of our fears rest on a solid foundation? It seems like most fears are unfounded, debilitating, and highly draining of our vital life energy. The beauty that lies hidden in fear can be found in the lessons it teaches us as we learn what is real and what is illusion, what is true and what is false, what needs to be let go of and what needs to be held firmly in the name of love.

Fear clothes itself in many ways, such as anxiety, panic, and full-out terror. It has been said in the books entitled *Conversations with God* by Neale Donald Walsh that fear is just False Evidence Appearing Real. I like that definition because, more often than not, it rings true. Most of what we fear never comes to be, even though it seems so real when we imagine it. The fear we experience can be unconscious and instinctual; it can also be learned and patterned as well as unlearned and re-patterned. I was exposed to some powerful lessons about fear when I became deeply aware of how I created a defence mechanism. I used this defence to make me feel "safe," which really wasn't a safety mechanism at all. My strategy related to food.

My husband is Italian, and the sharing of food and wine is paramount to him. It was a tragic disappointment when he made me a pizza in his wood-burning oven, and I became sick from eating it. He strongly believed that even though I claimed my top allergies to be wheat and dairy, I would someday at least be able to eat wheat and be okay. For a very long time, he offered to isolate himself with me in the mountains, feed me nothing but wheat-filled foods for a week, and support me while I got over whatever it was that was holding me back from being nourished by this grain. He understood and accepted the dairy allergy because I've had that one all my life (although he still encouraged me to try to desensitize to parmesan cheese), but since there have been various times when I've been able to tolerate wheat, he wanted to help me break through and expand my food choices in the name of pleasure, convenience, and overall culinary liberty.

Wheat and fear? Where am I going with this? They say hindsight is 20/20, and my sense of where my sensitivity to wheat comes from feels personally accurate. I heard a doctor once theorize that many allergies and sensitivities develop from an association made during a time of crisis. Her theory outlined how instead of being able to cope with the painful situation or emotion presenting itself, one begins to associate the trauma with the food or environmental substance closest at hand. The body becomes conditioned to believe that a particular material is a pathogen, a foreign particle, an "enemy" to be attacked or avoided completely. I can see now how I did this with wheat.

My family always went out to Italian restaurants (interesting that I should have found myself partnered with an Italian) and the main staple of our diet, like many North Americans, was wheat of various forms. At thirteen , when I started getting sick from what we later found out were parasites, I was told by a chiropractor that I had many toxins in my body and that I needed to alter my diet and eliminate many foods, including wheat. At this time, I felt constrained within the boundaries set upon me by my family, and this prescription for eating entirely different from them gave me an ability to establish an identity apart from my parents and sister, even if I felt unable to develop other healthy and unique ways of expressing myself. And so, by not eating wheat, by starting to cook for myself instead of participating in a familial and communal ritual of nourishment, by avoiding that which was symbolically a primal expression of who we were, I began to create a protective layer of armor that made me feel safe. I was attempting, subconsciously at the time, to shield myself from the inner agony of my family's secret dysfunctions, and to create my own sense of separate identity.

As with most defence mechanisms, that which once seemed to help make us "safe" causes us more pain in the end. As we become conscious of this dynamic, we get the chance to either maintain our defences and suffer, or to release them, find healing, and greater freedom. Luckily, life will keep bursting our fragile bubbles of illusion so that we get new chances to grow, heal, and thrive again. As I built my fortressed world as a teen, I gradually eliminated more foods from my diet until I could hardly eat anything without feeling sick. I literally couldn't digest life anymore. I even had a powerful dream during that time that my mother's apple pie, made with a wheat pastry crust, went into my body as the delicious pie that it was and became a sharp knife cutting me up inside as I tried to digest it—a very strong and painful image, and an apt one because this was how it felt to me when I would eat a "forbidden" food. I was unable to face what my pain was *really* about and the fears that *truly* ruled my life; therefore, I attached them to the most concrete, fundamental, and readily available thing I could (the food) in order to attempt to feel some sort of control over my life by avoiding the true source of my pain.

Now that I'm aware of the connection I created and that I am capable of changing, I can more honestly and courageously face the fears that lie beneath the defence, to heal and live more in truth. I am able to sustain a new relationship with my fears. And whether or not my body successfully digested wheat again became somewhat irrelevant—what was most important was the release from bondage and judgment. I continue to reintegrate all that lies beneath the surface; it is no longer about the food itself (which I now allow to be the neutral substance it was meant to be), but about the true struggle within to heal my wounds and create a more genuine sense of harmony with life as a whole. These days, as I eat wheat, I do so in a serene and grateful state of mind and being. Instead of focusing on how it might hurt me, I repeat a silent mantra inside, "Wheat is my friend" and imagine my body smiling as it digests the pasta, pizza, and other tasty treats. It's still a work in progress, and sometimes I can assimilate the wheat better than others. What I feel is that wheat is a very sensuous grain, earthy and grounding. Perhaps in the past I was afraid to let go into this sensation, because I had to face great pain in that place. And maybe now, as I embrace life as a whole, this is why I'm more able to take in things I used to judge as "bad" or "hurtful". Regardless, it is divine to not be so limited and to feel my body becoming stronger from within as my irrational fears dissolve, one by one.

Fears big and small

My experience with food and fear seems insignificant when I consider how many acts of violence and terror are committed in the world and how many people are paralyzed by very real fears on a daily basis. Every time the anniversary of 9/11 passes, I feel more and more humbled and saddened by the tragic losses that occurred on that day in 2001. I pray both for the souls of the American victims and their families and for the terrorist perpetrators and their families. Why do I include the latter? Because the terrorists must have been full of intense fear and hatred in order to plan, organize, and follow through on such acts of horrific violence. It reminds me that even though on a metaphysical level fear isn't real, in this flesh-and-blood world, some fears are very, very real.

The seeds of fear and the resulting acts of terror must be addressed at their source, and yet it is much more common to hear about reactive wars than responsive dialogues toward healing. Ignoring the root causes of hatred and maintaining a victim-perpetrator mentality feeds the cycle of violence and death when we should be working together for a better world. This is not an easy nor simple problem to solve, and yet with a common intention of resolution, I still choose to believe that all things are possible.

Other fears can be paralyzing, yet without a basis in actual reality. Many people suffer from panic attacks, fearful of dying when nothing truly is wrong except that the mind is taking them farther and farther in the direction of error rather than truth. I had a chance to explore this dynamic firsthand during a recent panic attack. I began taking two homeopathic remedies for my heart and nervous system. As often happens when taking such remedies, things get worse (sometimes a lot worse) before they get better. In this case, it took three days before I felt much of anything. Then, walking in Toronto one morning on the way to meet up with a friend, I began to feel shaky, my breath became short and shallow, and I felt a cold sweat coming on and a weakness taking over my muscles. Very soon that shakiness transformed into sheer panic, but I had the strength and consciousness this time to move through it more as a curious and compassionate observer rather than as a terrified victim. *Oh, there you are*, I thought. I knew something would surface from the depths in search of healing. Since I've experienced some intense panic attacks in my years, I was well aware that all hadn't been resolved so there was bound to be fear residue lurking in some dark, hidden caverns of my cellular structure.

Looking back, I recognize the greatest gift of that particular panic attack was my new awareness that the panic was truly just the fear of fear. If I connected with the fear that was surfacing and reminded myself that I could breathe, move through it, and that I was existentially *okay*, I knew that this too would pass. I wasn't really feeling afraid of anything in particular in that moment—it was just the vibration of fear having its way and needing some somatic space in order to be released. As I breathed my way through the panic, with every inhalation and exhalation I accepted the various sensations I was feeling and was able to release my fear of the fear. I imagined the fear inside me as a scared little child needing to be held and reassured, and from the solid place inside myself, I was able to nourish that petrified little girl. "It's okay. It's okay. You're okay." Little by little, the panic dissolved and the fear began to lessen until it dissipated, but I still felt kind of shaky throughout the day. Breathing and remembering what was true, that I was safe and could come to ease, became my high and holy practice of self-love. Gradually, love overcame fear, and I felt grounded and more at ease. Love always triumphs.

Through fear to love

Nothing that is unreal ever needs to be feared, including fear itself. *A Course in Miracles* states that nothing real can be threatened, and nothing unreal exists, and that within the acceptance of this one statement lays the entire peace of God. What does this mean? It tells us that real love, the truth of who we are, can never be destroyed, and that fear is actually not real, which takes away all sense of threat and need for defence. And how does this relate to our lives and our perceived reality where we *do* experience fear and it feels *very* real? The *Course* offers a brilliant way to understand this. Everything in life originates in one of two dynamics: fear or love. Every thought and every act is either an extension of love or a call for it. Which means, in very practical terms, that fear, when stripped bare, is a cry for love. If we were truly able to see life this way, wouldn't it be easier to have compassion for our fears and the fears of others, and to keep choosing love? Fear thus acts as a beautiful gift, a beacon of radiant light leading us back to the sanity and peace of love.

To illustrate how these principles work in "real life," I offer a personal example. There is a woman with whom I have struggled deeply over the years. Ours has not been a relationship that could be avoided easily or simply cast aside. Perhaps that is why she has been one of my biggest challenges in terms of coming from love rather than fear, and also setting healthy boundaries. In the early years of knowing and relating with one another, I felt tense dynamics between us, which seemed to only grow stronger as the years passed. On a certain level, I knew that she would be a big teacher for me if I allowed her to be. With each step of the way, if I remained honest and conscious enough within myself, I realized that I could either pass her off with negative judgments, shutting her out of my life because I believed she was undeserving of my time or energy, or I could go deeper in order to find greater healing for myself and potentially with her as well.

During the first few years of knowing one another, the conflicts between us intensified. I felt shocked by how malicious and mean-spirited she could be toward me, and I didn't know if there was any way to be in her presence and remain loving and honouring of myself. My obvious conclusion was that either she didn't like me or she must have felt threatened by me in some way—perhaps it was a mixture of the two. I felt attacked verbally and emotionally, and treated with a harshness that was shocking and hurtful. There was very little direct, honest communication between us; therefore, the feelings of hostility and bitterness were ongoing. Looking at this situation with a limited and fear-based vision, I could only see that she was unfair to me in those years, judging and attacking me in a way that was highly destructive. And based on the messages I was receiving from her, she felt that I was being equally hurtful to her, even if I didn't see it that way. It was clear that if we both remained limited in our perspective, we might stay stuck forever in attack and defence, each of us playing the vicious roles of victim and perpetrator, neither one of us ever breaking free from this powerless state.

The dynamics between us got worse before they got better, and over time there were harsh words, hurt feelings, and many, many tears on my part—and possibly on her part, too. There have been times when I refused to speak to or see her because I considered the energy directed toward me to be abusive and manipulative. I was working hard on loving myself and valuing my worth and felt the need to protect myself from further pain. But as long as my boundary was based in fear, in this state of "cut off," love kept calling me to grow by changing my perspective and seeing beyond my limited vision.

Eventually, the anger and hatred inside me, based in fear, made me physically ill. I developed a very nasty and out-of-control case of Candidiasis, a chronic yeast infection due to an overgrowth of bad bacteria in the gut. My condition became so severe and debilitating that one day, during a Reiki level two training in Montreal, I collapsed in agony on the floor with extremely painful abdominal cramps. My compassionate teacher hovered over me whispering, "Pardonnez, pardonnez," which is the French equivalent of "Forgive, forgive." At that time, I wasn't ready or willing to face the underlying dynamic of fear and lack of forgiveness that had overtaken me. In my judgments, I saw her as bad. I feared that I was bad, but in reality, it was my own limitations on love that were 'bad', if anything was to be labeled that way.

I couldn't continue with my Reiki training that day. I left my teacher's home and headed straight to a hospital emergency ward to find out what was physiologically wrong with me, still trying to convince myself that my pain had *nothing* to do with the relational conflicts and how they were eating me up inside. As time passed and I tended to the physical aspects of bringing myself back into balance, I became willing to explore and surrender the psychological dynamics that had me imprisoned by my own stubborn resistance to letting go. I also continued to gain inspiration from *A Course in Miracles* as I sought some wise psycho-spiritual guidance about how to heal core relationships that felt so steeped in fear, so devoid of love, so traumatic to my tender and sensitive self. I began putting my hand on my heart and taking several deep, full breaths before being in her presence, trying to come from a loving place no matter what energy I was met with.

Over the years, and with lots of counseling and personal growth work, I came to see this enemy-and-teacher-in-disguise in a whole new light—a more compassionate and loving light, a less painful light. I started to practice being a witness to her dynamics instead of simply reacting to them from my own storehouse of fears. It wasn't easy. With each time new attack, I felt hurt and had to stop myself from reacting. My success rate hasn't been perfect, to say the least, but I accept each phase of learning. I have worked on letting go of needing the relationship to be something other than what it is and what it has become. As I practice deep acceptance of things just as they are, I give much less emotional energy to the conflictive dance I have been a part of. I let go. I am less scared. I have a lot less to lose. I am not as attached as I used to be. My suffering has decreased exponentially, thank God.

As I worked on healing and releasing my fears, I witnessed my inner changes creating external results. There were fewer confrontations, fights, and hurts. The healing was far from complete, however. I realized that we had times of greater openness with one another only when I learned what to say, what not to say, and how to be with her in a way that engendered fewer attacks. It was nice to be able to connect in a much less hostile, much more respectful way, and yet my heart continued to beat faster when I connected with her, because I was aware that at any moment I could be attacked again. There was also work for me to do in terms of taking responsibility for where I was putting up walls between us and, at times, putting forward energy that was less than loving. We are each accountable for our half of the whole relationship.

As I become much more solid within myself and the life I am living, and as I continue to receive her sharpness and anger, I do my best to not take it as personally as I used to; I don't shrink and become small or react and become defensive. I am learning about healthy boundaries, and I remain curious about the dynamics of this relationship that calls me both to see beyond my fear and to honour my worth, no matter what. I accept the challenge. I embrace the learning. I practice loving what is. And this time, when it comes time to choose how much of my vital life energy I give to this relationship, my choice comes much more from love than from fear. I am not doing her any favours by allowing her to treat me in such a hurtful way. And I love myself by saying *no* to the unhealthy dynamics. I continue to learn and grow in all my relations. As the channeled spirit guide Emmanuel says, the journey of life itself is a movement, a dance "through fear to love in an imperfect world." Let's all keep dancing, shall we?

Beauty tips for fear

1. Get to know your personal fear messaging system as it shows up in your physical body. With curiosity and compassion, observe how fear speaks to you through the voice of sensations related to anxiety, panic, dread, etc. What is your body trying to whisper (or scream) to you? What does it long for you to know? If you could hear its voice of guidance, what would it say? Are you able to listen? What does your whole being need from you in order to shift the fear into love without bypassing the tough stuff?

2. As you get in touch with the sensations of fear, begin to breathe big acceptance into them. Breathe with that shallow, shaky breath. Breathe right into the knot in your stomach, the light-headedness, the racing heart, the lump in your throat. Make big space for how your fear is showing up. To repress it and limit its space serves only to increase fear to seemingly out-of-control proportions. Allow a part of you that is still solid and grounded in truth (i.e. the witness), to give you a greater chance at not being overwhelmed by your fear. That part of you might be as big as your spine, as vast as your belly, or as small as your pinky toe. The size of your solid self isn't as important as the fact that you still have one—and everyone does somewhere—even if it feels like it has been reduced to what feels like a single cell.

3. Make a "Top 10" list of your greatest fears, without censoring anything. Then grab a mirror, look yourself in the eyes, and affirm (meaning it as much as you can—the "fake it 'til you make it" rule applies here if necessary):

   "Even if _____ [insert whatever it is you

fear] happens, I love and accept myself fully and I rest in the knowledge that I am okay."

This will help you remember that you are always more than the conditions of your life, regardless of how they show up, shift, and change.

4. The next time you find yourself acting out (e.g., addictively drinking or using drugs) or acting in (e.g., isolation or depression), feeling or being reactive, defensive and/or shut down, take a moment to connect with your inner self by taking a few deep belly breaths, and ask yourself the following questions:

"What am I afraid of right now?"

"What do I not want to feel?"

When we block, resist, or give into fearful feelings, we are more susceptible to losing track of life's beauty, and we remain lost in the static of life rather than singing and dancing to the music of our soul. As we accept our fears, offer compassion for them, and explore their source, we are no longer in the grip of their irrational power over us. When we can feel the full range of our feelings, we are free. Awakening to love means we have a new and powerful relationship with our fears that help to connect us with our feelings and remind us that we always have a choice as to whether we give in to those fears or overcome them by choosing love again and again. Here's another great question to ask:

"What would love think/say/feel/do?" Listen for an answer, and then try it.

Chapter 9

The Beauty of Gratitude

"Love is the way I walk in gratitude."
A Course in Miracles (Lesson 195)

"Just for today, I give thanks for my many blessings."
Reiki Principle #3

Gratitudinal vibrations

I attended a lecture by the famous scientist/mystic Gregg Braden a few years ago in which he shared the results of studies proving that gratitude is the highest possible energy we can experience in this life. Research was done to measure the vibration of various emotions such as love, anger, hate, hope, and sadness (to name a few) to determine the rate at which they resonate and also how bacteria and viruses behave in their midst. The results were both predictable and surprising. Braden shared that what we consider base, negative emotions such as resentment, hatred, bitterness, and anger all carry a very low vibration, and that bacteria and viruses thrive in their presence. More positive, nourishing emotions such as generosity, love, and gratitude vibrate at a distinguishably higher rate, and bacteria and viruses have trouble surviving while these emotions are the active forces at play. In simple terms, those are the more predictable and understandable conclusions of this research.

But the big surprise was the quality that achieved the highest rate of vibration, the one that was the most resistant to disease: Gratitude. Love was definitely right up there on the list of high emotional states, but in the end, giving thanks won top prize.

What is it about being grateful that is so incredibly powerful? I think it has to do with the normally dissatisfied ego mind that is often brilliant at finding reasons why everything is not okay just as it is. We're missing this, we don't have enough of that, if only we had this we would be perfectly happy, or if only we didn't have that problem, life would be fabulous. You get the picture. Instead of being content and thankful for all the blessings we already *do* have, our crazy fear-based mind would rather stew over the scarcity and lack that it perceives as our human fate, leaving little to no room for the abundance that comes from being grateful for all things, big and small, here and now.

No complaints

A homeless man I used to see regularly on my street when I lived in the West End of Vancouver caught my attention long before we spoke. He would sit quietly on the park bench, dirty and disheveled, teeth rotting, hair long, knotted, and greasy, wearing the same clothes day after day. But it was not the details of his external appearance that made a distinct impression on me. Beneath the dirt and grunge were these beautiful eyes and this bright smile that spoke of a man with a rich history and a valuable present, with an intriguing personal story that I didn't know but could instinctively sense through his bafflingly serene and contented demeanor. Unlike the other homeless people I encountered, he never asked for anything in all the time I saw him there on the bench and strolling through the neighborhood. He smiled with respect and a sense of dignity that diametrically opposed his looks, his circumstances, and the many labels that society's prejudices and discriminations would immediately give him.

One day I broke the ice and said more than hello. I asked him his name and offered some information about myself based on his questions. His name was Ken, and he was specifically interested in what I was doing in Vancouver because he had also studied psychology many years ago at a university in Western Canada. He told me bits and pieces of his story: He had lived with his sister for a while not far from where we were, but then she died and he was now on his own. I still don't know why he ended up living on the street instead of making his way into a home after his sister's passing, or why he continued in that kind of street-living existence.

All I know from my experience of Ken is that every day, whether it was raining (as it often did in Vancouver) or the sun was shining brightly, he expressed gratitude for the beauty of the day. When I asked him how he was doing, he would always reply, "No complaints." Really? How amazing is that? In my comfortable little apartment with all my food, shelter, and basic needs met, working, studying, and living in the direction of my dreams, I could always find something to complain about. Every time I heard him speak his wise mantra, "No complaints," I was stopped in my tracks and remembered that I had a great deal to learn from Ken.

The light of gratitude

There was a time in my life where everything seemed lost. Actually, there have been a few times. Once in Montreal, I went to a prayer vigil with one of my friends from the Religious Studies faculty. We were instructed to light a candle in the center of the circle as a symbol of our life force, our hope, our spirits, our heart-prayers. I lit my candle, knowing I was desperately in need of some light in my life. As I returned to my seat, a gentle breeze moved through the room in just the right way and blew out one single glowing flame—mine. As I watched my light extinguish, I saw it as a mirror for exactly how I felt. My light had gone out. The wax and the wick were still there, and the many other lights nearby could reignite my candle at a moment's notice. But all I could see was that smoldering flame, the smoke dancing its way upward until there was just a cold, dark, empty space around what was briefly warm and lit. I was pretty deep in despair, and gratitude felt a long way off.

A few years later, I was in even worse shape. I had just finished a treatment to help cleanse me of my higher than high mercury load (I had more than double the highest level of mercury my environmental specialist doctor had ever seen in a human being), and the treatment itself nearly killed me. After being injected with the chelating drug DMPS and not getting any kind of boost afterward to replace the vitamins and minerals lost in the detoxification process, I was a mess—and that is truly a major understatement. I had sharp pain in my kidneys, I was constantly anxious and shaky, I couldn't sleep or rest, and little by little the toxicity that was building up because my body couldn't release the mercury fast enough re-poisoned me. I felt trapped in my body with no sign of relief, and I understood all too well why in times past mercury poisoning was called the "Mad Hatter's Disease" because I felt completely crazy.

I did everything in my power to re-balance myself, but nothing worked. I ate simply and lightly in a way my body usually responded well to. I meditated, visualized, and practiced yoga. I talked to my counsellor and my friends for encouragement and connection. I took homeopathic and herbal remedies. Finally, when none of these attempts did any good, I broke down and called a woman named Mary, a Catholic nun who is anything but traditional. She practices Reiki, Cranio-Sacral therapy, and Polarity work. I knew I needed some serious help, and since she seemed to have a powerful pipeline to God, she was the one I went to for a healing session. I lay on her massage table, surrounded by paintings of saints, angels, and such, and listened to her call in Mother Mary, Jesus, Buddha, and other Archangels who might be of divine assistance. Then I waited.

I felt the warmth of her hands, yet I still couldn't calm my anxiety or soothe my irritated mind. I had no conscious sense of energy being transferred through her humble and loving hands. *If this doesn't work, what on earth can I do next?* I wondered. At the end of the session, I honestly shared with Mary that I still felt horrible and didn't know what to do for myself. She had one word to offer me: *gratitude*. She gave me a "gratitude prescription," saying that even if it seemed crazy to be thankful when so much was going "wrong" for me, the smallest act of gratitude could move mountains.

I was willing to try anything at that point. That night, in the midst of another restless and angst-ridden attempt at sleep, I decided to give Mary's suggestion a try. I realized that it might not get any better for me. Perhaps this was it. Maybe this was all the energy and health I would ever have, and instead of fighting against this reality, it was time to be thankful for *all I did have*. And so, I surrendered. Even if I were destined to live with this anxiety, pain, and low energy, I would create something good and beautiful with my life. I thought of all the people I was thankful for—including those I love with relative ease and also loved ones who challenge me deeply. I felt only love and gratitude for them all in that moment, because to feel anything else simply added to my suffering. I was thankful for the life I had instead of longing for everything to be different. I chose to love my life as it was, and if things improved, that would be great. If not, that was okay too.

Amazingly, in this letting go into an experience of true and raw gratitude, everything did begin to shift. I fell asleep that night, for the first time in a few weeks, and actually got some peaceful rest. Little by little, as I cherished what energy I had, I was able to gain some strength. By the sweet grace of God, I began to work part-time as a receptionist at a yoga studio and became part of a community that continues to be one of the biggest blessings of my life. The first step on my healing journey was that of gratitude.

I am a living testament to the validity of Gregg Braden's experiments and Ken's beautiful life philosophy of "No Complaints." I am infinitely grateful that I learned to practice gratitude before it was too late. And I continue to exercise my gratitude muscles when I start to feel down, or when I focus on what I don't have or what I'm not experiencing, and in general when I forget how many blessings I have, taking far too much for granted. Gratitude changes our mind from lack to abundance, from scarcity to fullness, from misery to happiness, from suffering to peace. Not bad for something that is available to us in every single, conscious moment of thanks for all that *is*. In truth, all that is seen through the eyes of gratitude shines with beauty.

Beauty tips for gratitude

1. For one week, as you awaken in the morning and also as you prepare to sleep at night, jot down five things you are especially grateful for. They can be people, places, events, circumstances—they can be big or small—just list them. Notice how you feel during that gratitude week.

2. When you are feeling down and possibly wallowing in self-pity or despair, take a moment to breathe gratitude for just one thing. It could be that the sun is shining or that a friend just called. It could be anything. Allow gratitude to be the antidote for any and all spirit crushers.

3. Say "thank you." I mean, really say it. As you move through your day, when you would normally pass by people as if they weren't your brothers and sisters (e.g., the man who receives your subway tokens, the check-out person at the grocery store, the woman who just gave you your mail, etc.), look that person in the eyes and genuinely say "thank you." Let them know that their way of being of service in the world has touched your life. You will be reminding them that they matter. This is a big gift.

4. Take a moment to close your eyes and bring awareness into your body. Often we notice only the things that are going wrong inside us, the pains, discomforts, stresses, and tensions. In this moment, bring awareness to all that is going *right* in your body—all that is in harmony and at ease. You don't need to specifically be aware of the biology of it all—just notice how much is working well inside you and thank your Creator for the gift and miracle of your life. You are breathing, your heart is beating—a myriad of miraculous life processes are happening without your conscious control. This is no small feat.

Part IV:

Honouring the Beauty of the North

We turn our awakening hearts to the North and we give great thanks for:
Permission to hibernate
Winter fun and warm nights by the fire
Cozying up and cozying in
Celebrations of light in dark times
Rituals of peace and joy
A time to reflect and remember and reunite
The wonder and joy of children living the magic
First snow like a shower of pure diamonds
Snow angels
Long walks on frozen lakes
The earthy, green smell of pine trees
Light birthing
Enduring with hope
Making peace with all that is and resolving for the best
Patiently, ceaselessly awaiting new life
HO!

Chapter 10

The Beauty of Grief

"The risk of love is loss, and the price of loss is grief—
But the pain of grief
Is only a shadow
When compared with the pain
Of never risking love."
Hilary Stanton Zunin

"Give sorrow words. The grief that does not speak whispers the o'er-frought heart, and bids it break."
~ William Shakespeare

Grief roots

In my life, I have often felt a deep and wide grief, yet I have lacked a clear, conscious grasp of its source. Where could this incredibly powerful grief come from? How could I have accumulated so much sadness? Compared to other lives on this planet, what would warrant such streams of salty tears on my part? Grief, stripped bare, needs no specific conditions for its existence. It simply is. The magnitude of another's tragedy does not diminish the grief each of us might experience inside. Sometimes it has a cause that we are well aware of, and other times grief simply shows up and asks to be given its due space.

Often I have sensed my grief to be so big, so powerful, so all-encompassing that I have gone into addiction/obsession/compulsion mode just to avoid feeling what I was feeling. Instead of being able to bear the original wound for what it was, I created a new problem to focus upon. This allowed me to avoid feeling the deeper pain. I would run from one relationship to the next, thinking that if I could only find "Mr. Right" it would all be okay; I wouldn't need to be so sad anymore. Or perhaps if I smoked this herbal cigarette out of sheer rebellion, I would get my power back and the grief would dissolve in the smoke fumes. Or if I ate a few more tortilla chips, I would be so full there would be no more room for feeling at all.

At times, when I was sick with Chronic Fatigue Syndrome, I would let myself cry and cry and cry. Then I would become even more exhausted, my eyes would sting for days, and I would decide then and there it was better not to cry. But really it all just got stored up for later release. And sometimes, when I felt deeply sad and the tears were ready to rush up, out, and all over the place, I would sense that if I started to cry I would never, ever stop. I was quite convinced that the infinity of my grief was altogether possible.

I had my reasons for feeling sad. In addition to experiencing chronic illness in my youth, there was loss in my life. At times, there was lots of loss. And one of the biggest losses was the breakup of my family, which was so painful to digest that I chose (for the most part) to numb out rather than feel it. My pain at that time threw me into a major downward spiral that had me questioning almost everything I held to be true and good while growing up. The following example is interesting, partly because it shows how I tended to attach emotional wounds to food.

I used to absolutely *adore* my mother's chocolate rum balls that she made for Christmas. Right after my dad left, shortly after New Year's Day of 1995, I brought a bag of the rum balls to my new home in Montreal. They stayed in that Ziploc bag in the fridge for months. I would take them out and smell their heavenly aroma, but I wouldn't eat them. I wouldn't dare take a bite. I couldn't take that goodness in. It was too symbolic of what I remembered of the togetherness of our family, and with that now gone, chocolate rum balls were out of the question. If I didn't taste their goodness, I wouldn't have to feel the full extent of my grief.

Surrendering to grief: feeling the feelings

For many years after my parents' break-up, I worked to heal my life on multiple levels. I enrolled in a three-year counsellor training course and master's degree program in Langley, British Columbia, at a school called Clearmind. A clear mind would be a welcome change. The training at this institution is highly experiential, based on the belief that we must dive deep into our own healing journey in order to be able to hold space for, and effectively facilitate, anyone else doing the same. During my first year, I dated (and at times obsessed) my way through the program. I dated a man in each of the first-year classes: day class, night class, and the Vancouver Island class.

My chaotic and neurotic love life was, for better or worse, on display, up for observation and analysis (and some criticism, triggered by my siren-like behavior) by the whole community. It was not easy, to say the least. I was highly encouraged by my wise and seasoned teachers to take a break from men, a "mancation." Their theory was that I was distracting myself from feeling and healing some emotional wounds through my addictive behavior in intimate relationships. If I would take a real break from men, I would apparently get a chance to feel my deeper feelings and move through them. One benefit of doing so might be the cessation of painful and damaging patterns with the men in my life—a cycle of pain, loss, and disappointment I kept putting myself and others through. It was a great idea, but not one I was ready for until partway through my second year in the course, a time when things got so bad that I hit cold, rock-hard bottom. At that point, I was willing to consider anything.

I wanted to be in charge of determining the duration of my "mancation," and my choice was forty days and forty nights. I figured if I was going to do it, why not be biblical about it? At least that would be a good start, and I always had the option to extend it. I uttered a sincere prayer at the beginning of my vacation from men and am highly grateful that it was answered affirmatively. I asked God to take away my attraction to men. Remove my libido. Don't allow me to fall for anyone, because I don't want to be distracted. Done deal. And it worked. Absolutely *nothing* and *no one* showed up in terms of any possible suitors, obsessions, or fantasy men on my part, to the point that at the end of the "mancation," I wondered if I would *ever* be attracted to anyone again! But the core purpose for this experience was more important than any fear I had of future consequences.

The most important part of my "mancation" is what happened in that first phase of withdrawing from my distractions. Without the obsession of men—past, present, or future—I was unbelievably *bored*. With the majority of my energy and time devoted to my studies and work, my creative juices were flowing. But down-time was like dropping into a big black hole of nothingness. One day, I chose to explore that boredom and see what lay beneath it, instead of bemoaning the fact that life without my incessant relationship dramas felt incredibly dull.

As I lay in bed, I imagined myself floating in Lake Boredom—a deep, vast space that seemed to engulf me. Instead of fighting it or doing anything I could to avoid it, I surrendered. And as I did, I began to feel big emotions. One of the most powerful emotions to surface was grief. As I dropped into my emotional field, I felt a deep well of sadness, and mostly it had to do with the loss of my family. I realized I had never truly let myself feel the depth of this particular sadness. I cried many rivers of tears. I let myself remember all the tough and painful moments when I felt threatened and out of control as so much crumbled before my eyes. The tears flowed freely as I recalled all the lies, betrayals, guilt, pain, confusion, and fear.

As I let go into this seemingly empty space, what I found was a fullness of many parts of myself starting to come back together into an integrated whole. I both witnessed it in myself and lived it by feeling my way through it. And as I let myself grieve all that loss, an extraordinary thing happened: I started to feel, for the first time in a very, very long time, the beauty of my family. I felt the true love I had for each one of them, and the love I remember us all sharing together. I recalled many sweet times in my life growing up where I felt loved and a sense of belonging, where we laughed and joked together and all seemed right in the world. Those were precious times. I had lost them somehow when I wasn't willing to face, feel, and move through the genuine path of my grief. In that moment, if I had a rum ball beside me, I believe I would have had the courage and the grace to take a bite, to let it fill my hungry belly, and to smile, filled with all the sweetness and all the bitterness—perfect in the balance of it all.

Love and loss

Grief is beautiful simply because it is real, simply because we feel it. We don't grieve what we haven't loved and lost, or what we don't feel deeply for. And any love given and received in this life, whether present or past, is beautiful. One of my most intense experiences of grief involved the loss of a very dear friend. The dedication to this book honours Nicole, a precious and vivacious human being who died a sudden and shocking death in a car accident in Australia. She was my soul sister. We had met eight years previous in a gymnasium in Montreal, where we were both auditioning to be part of Mosaica, McGill University's modern dance ensemble. There was an immediate spark of connection between us, a blissful recognition of a kindred spirit. Luckily, we both made the cut, and for three years we danced, played, laughed, and cried together.

Nicole was a little younger than me, since I was at McGill as a mature student, and yet we got along famously as we participated in each other's choreographed dances and checked in with one other during summers apart. I savoured every moment I got to spend with her because she was so full of life, love, and passion, which she awakened in me. She truly danced from her core, which was a steady and powerful stream of beauty that moved and inspired me like nothing else. I can still envision her now in my mind's eye, dancing with captivating grace and strength.

After completing my bachelor's degree at university, I spent three years working in Toronto until finally I was ready to do a master's degree. To Nicole's absolute delight, I decided to go to school in Vancouver, where she was working toward a Naturopathic Doctor degree. We had the great fortune to live together downtown, right by the ocean. It was a friendship love affair of the first degree. We were fully supportive of one another's dreams and were the first to champion the other through every aspect of growth experienced during that time. So many kitchen-table conversations were had over men, boys, more men, and more boys. She longed to find someone to love and be loved by in a way that honoured the goddess that she was, yet it was rare for her to find a man who could really meet her intensity. There were many struggles we saw one another through, as well as oh, so many joys.

After Nicole finished her Naturopathic degree, she was exhausted by the many years of nearly constant schooling, was in great need of feeding her vibrant spirit, and felt drawn to spend a year Down Under. Even though her family had a sense of foreboding about her Australia trip from the beginning, and they were concerned about her not stepping immediately into a naturopathic practice, finding a home, and taking responsibility for supporting herself and moving forward in her adult life, she needed some time to be free and *just live.* She had been studying and taking exams for what felt like an eternity and needed a taste of freedom and something different before she made any further commitments.

Nicole excitedly explored options for adventure, and in the end she felt thrilled to go to Australia to travel and work for a year. In those months before she left, I felt like I was already losing her. Maybe it was just that she was free in a whole new way, and her energy was already moving beyond Vancouver and her old life; yet something told me that she was really going away, and I didn't experience her the way I used to. I witnessed these changes with as much trust and detachment as I could, and I just kept loving her and celebrating the next steps in her life path.

The last night I saw Nicole before her trip, we got together at my new apartment, which held many of her furnishings that she lent to me for my final year of school. I lovingly made her a delicious dinner and we watched a few episodes of *Lost* for old time's sake. We ate our favourite date squares for dessert. We joked a little bit, ironically, that she was going to Australia, departure point of the *Lost* plane before it crashed. We laughed as we both prayed that she wouldn't get "lost," neither of us really believing anything bad could happen to her. This chapter in her life was all too good and exciting to be ruined in any way. She deserved every ounce of happiness and not a single trace of tragedy.

I received various e-mails from Nicole as she recounted her adventures, and she did indeed live it up. Skydiving, surfing, bungee jumping—you name it, she was saying a big fat "YES!" to it all. That included her explorations with some lovely new young men. Her e-mails carried a sense of the Nicole I knew and loved, who chatted with me at the kitchen table on so many occasions. She had a met a special man and felt drawn to travel with him to Ayers Rock. She was seeking my opinion, because she had been travelling for over a month at that point and was supposed to settle down and live with a host family and begin working. But she *really* liked this man and it was a great opportunity to travel to this sacred site. She wondered what my thoughts were on the subject.

I was very busy at that time with trying to finish my master's degree, writing my thesis, and working to support myself; it was rare for me to spare a moment to respond at length to any e-mail. But I'm happy to say that in this instance I did, because it ended up being the last message Nicole received from me while she was alive. I sat in the internet café, read her words slowly and carefully, and took my time responding to her, offering her my heartfelt love and support. The essence of my response to Nicole was that she was in Australia to really live and enjoy her experiences, and if she was able to postpone her work for a little while longer, why not say "YES!" to this adventure too? I encouraged her to follow her heart and her vivacious spirit and to do what felt best. I had a hunch that would mean going on the journey to Ayers Rock, which is exactly what she did.

A week later, I received an e-mail and phone message from an ex-boyfriend who went to Nicole's school. He was checking in with me to see if I was okay. I felt confused—why would I *not* be okay? Was he thinking that I was still suffering from our break-up, which had happened more than a year ago? I was not. It was very kind of him to think of me, though. But my assumption was wrong. He knew of Nicole's tragic accident and wanted to make sure I was okay because he knew how much I loved that girl. Hearing the news over the phone, I went into full-fledged shock. No. No! NO! It couldn't be possible. Not Nicole. Not my soul sister, my darling friend I held in my arms and comforted so many times in her moments of distress, the woman who promised to be a bridesmaid in my wedding one day. It couldn't be. There must have been a colossal, universal mistake.

I no longer felt my body. It was all I could do to keep breathing. Immediately, I called people I loved to let them know what had happened and to ask for help and support. My grief was too big for me to face alone, and I was well aware of that fact. My whole world had changed forever without Nicole in it, and I felt the overwhelming loss immediately and fully. Every morning that week, I had been waking up around 4:00 or 4:30 a.m. with a feeling of doom and anxiety and had no idea why. Now I knew.

My life was consumed with thoughts and feelings about Nicole for a long time after that dreadful day. I learned from her father, who had contacted psychics to help him understand what happened to Nicole's spirit at the time of her death, she too believed it was a huge mistake when her spirit body stood beside her lifeless physical body on the side of the Australian road. I can imagine her standing there, arms crossed in utter defiance, saying, "Oh no. No way. Put me back. I am *so* not done with this life!"

The psychics also shared that the spirit of her grandmother came to assist her in transitioning to the other side, and that Nicole was to be part of a healing force for the planet, just not in the way she had anticipated. It was an honour for her to be part of this group of healing spirits, apparently. I felt somewhat comforted to think of Nicole joining the force from beyond in a divinely appointed mission, because it was truly in her nature to bring love, beauty, and healing to all that she touched. And yet, from my very vulnerable, humble, and selfish human side, I still wanted her here with me, with us, for at least six or seven more decades to come. I missed her already. I will miss her always on this earth.

Big, conscious, magic grief

The dance of my grief over Nicole's loss was a powerful experience for me without the distractions I used to create before my lessons in counsellor training and my "mancation." I could love myself through the sadness. I was feeling the pain in all of its extremities and subtleties and was able to share my experiences and keep inhaling and exhaling through it all. Above all, I cherished the love I had for Nicole and the beauty of our friendship while allowing this experience to move me, change me, and deepen me in ways I would never have imagined. I allowed magic to touch my experience of her passing, just as my life had become more enchanted with her in it. I found beauty in my grief because it was grounded in the purity of my love.

As I surrendered to the current of grief that shifted on a moment-to-moment basis, the magic showed up. I believe that it is when we become so raw and undefended in life, when we are struck by tragedy or crisis, we are able to open up and really see the miracles all around us as the voice of God speaks in highly creative ways. Usually we are too busy or distracted to listen. But when we are laid bare in our emotions at the core of our being, the awakening comes. I went for a massage one day with my dear friend, Cindi, knowing that I needed the comfort of touch to help ground me in my body. At certain points during the massage, I felt that it was Nicole working on me, not Cindi. I sensed Nicole's love and energy being channeled through Cindi in order to touch me with tenderness one last time.

And just as I felt that to be true, Cindi felt it also, which she shared with me at the end of the session. We both cried; I felt so grateful, moved, and blessed to know such a love that lives and moves beyond the veil between worlds.

Then came the flickering of lights. Nicole, when on this earth, had an ability to turn lights on and off just by walking past them. Whatever it was about her, she had an electrical charge that created this phenomenon. She told me about this gift of hers when we lived together in Vancouver, and one night, at dusk, on the way to our favorite sushi restaurant, I had the pleasure of witnessing it. As we walked side by side, street lights that were previously on turned off, and vice versa. And now, with Nicole having passed away, I found the lights in my bedroom turning on and off with great regularity. I checked the bulb to see if it was loose or dying. Neither was the case. The light would flicker on and off when I most needed to feel her near. And I would say out loud, "Hi Nicole!" I still, in moments of inspiration, whisper, "I love you, Nicole," and I believe she hears me. A few months after Nicole's death, her mother, Mai, told me that she was visiting with her sister in Edmonton. As they shared memories about Nicole, the lights began to go on and off for no reason and they felt her presence. I asked if she was familiar with Nicole's "gift" of turning lights on and off while in the physical world. Mai never knew of this. As we spoke, there was a hint of recognition that Nicole was speaking to us via the other world just to remind us, through the vehicle of light, that life lives on.

About a week after Nicole's passing and a few days before her memorial service, I was preparing for school when, for the first time since her death, I felt anger replace the deep and utter sadness, which was triggered by something my partner said on the phone. We both knew that my anger was not really toward or about him—it was stemming from my feeling that it wasn't fair that Nicole was gone, and I was angry at whomever and whatever took her from me, from us. In that moment, the song "What a Wonderful World" by Louis Armstrong came on the radio. As I listened and took in its words and meaning, I was not in agreement. It did not feel like a wonderful world to me—not without Nicole in it. That day at school I was to act as a mentor, assisting others who were in the first-year counsellor training program with an exercise called the Fairy Tale. They were to write about their struggle in an imaginative and creative manner, and to write all the way to resolution. I didn't know how I could possibly be of much assistance that day, not in my negative state of mind and being, but I did my best.

One of the young men I was assisting shared his saga of addiction and lack of belonging by assuming the voice of an out-of-tune guitar string. As he shared his struggle through this analogy, his resolution involved discovering that what he thought was out of tune was actually a sharp note that was needed in combination with the whole in order to create beautiful music. As he read his story out loud, my heart began to soften and melt, and tears welled up in my eyes. I felt such compassion for the pain we humans experience in this world. I was in awe of this young man who was showing such bravery in choosing to find a way to heal rather than drown in the undertow of his addiction. At the end of his fairy tale, his conclusion brought him to join the other guitar strings, each with their own unique sound and tone, in playing his song: "What a Wonderful World." I couldn't believe it, and yet it was divine. It was as if I could feel Nicole's hand gently resting on my shoulder, reminding me not to give in to bitter despair. There is so much pain, loss, grief, sadness, and tragedy in this life, but it is still a wonderful world. This courageous young man's fairy tale was a magical, miraculous, and beautiful reminder.

The synchronicities revealing beauty in grief didn't end there. I spoke at the memorial for Nicole at the naturopathic college she had graduated from, sharing the love and gratitude I felt for this amazing woman who touched my life so richly and deeply. At another memorial service held by the family, I listened to various family members speak of their love for Nicole, of her brilliant, captivating, and adventuresome spirit, and I just cried. I couldn't imagine that my being was able to contain much more sadness. When the floor was opened to anyone else who wished to speak in remembrance of

Nicole, I chose to stay quiet because I had had my turn a few days before.

After the first woman spoke of her beautiful experience in knowing Nicole, the master of ceremonies took his place at the front of the hall, looked out into the many faces staring back at him, and asked with curiosity: "Who is Lori?" I imagine Nicole's family had let him know how close we were and that I might want to share a few words. I don't remember how my body got from my seat to the front of the room. Magnetically drawn, I felt like I floated there, and as I stood before the multitude of people gathered out of pure love for Nicole, I couldn't stop crying long enough to say one word. I looked over to Nicole's aunt, a very loving and spiritual woman, and she whispered to me: "Breathe." I tried. Then, breath by breath, I sensed Nicole's voice urging me on, saying, "You can do it," and again I felt that warm, soothing hand on my shoulder.

I began to share what flowed naturally from my heart. I have no recollection of exactly what I said, but I remember sharing how I met Nicole, speaking of the friendship we nurtured over the years, and giving thanks for the many ways in which she blessed my life. I was about finished when I felt the urge to tell these beautiful, grieving people about "What a Wonderful World." I turned to the master of ceremonies to see if I could take up a bit more time, and he said I could have all the time I needed. I proceeded to tell the fairy tale story and felt the power of what I was offering vibrating throughout the room. They could feel the magic too. And the magic just kept growing.

A lovely woman came up to me after the service and asked if I had any idea how much that story touched a whole row of people. I was uncertain what she meant until she said that when Nicole danced in Vancouver, just before I met her in Montreal, she performed one final choreographed dance in a recital, and it was to the song "What a Wonderful World." Incredible. Then I met the woman who had choreographed that very dance. Shivers ran all through my body. I had no previous knowledge of that dance. More and more, I felt that even though Nicole had past from this earth, she wasn't really gone.

One more time

In the weeks following Nicole's death, I went through many stages of grief. In addition to experiencing amazing synchronicities like the ones I have shared, I underwent a major shaking up of my ideas about life. I had always held a belief that everything happens for a reason, for a greater purpose—sometimes we have an inkling of what that might be and sometimes we are completely in the dark. In this case, a part of me continued to feel like there had been a blip in the universe, a colossal error, and that everything might have a purpose except this. I could not digest the reality of losing Nicole nor believe that anything positive could come of it. It was just wrong. God must have made a mistake—my rational, grieving mind imagined that maybe he was looking the other way for an instant, or perhaps her angels were taking a short break—but this couldn't possibly be part of any benevolent divine plan.

On December 31 of that year, I felt immense sadness and despair that was nearly unbearable. There was none of the usual gratitude for the year that had passed or excitement for the fresh year to come. It was all doom and gloom, deeper than ever. I found out later that was the day Nicole's lifeless body was delivered to Vancouver from Australia. That night, I was in our restaurant in Costa Rica, feeling like I needed desperately to contact Nicole. I couldn't keep all these heavy emotions inside and longed to reach out to her, some way, somehow. So I sat by myself while everyone celebrated and wrote Nicole an e-mail, sending it to her usual address. In that message, I let her know how much I loved her and how very much I missed her. I asked her questions about where she was that I knew were unlikely to ever be answered on this earth plane. I let her know what was going on in my life—what I was up to and all that I was feeling. It was a friendly check-in. Just before I clicked "send," I told Nicole how much I wished I could hear from her one more time—please, just one more time. I sent the message, comforted somewhat from the belief that, on some level, she got it.

Shortly after I arrived home to Vancouver about a week later, I retrieved a stack of mail from my landlord that he had been holding for me while I was away. I was en route to work, so I began opening the first envelope as I walked down the street. I stopped in my tracks, frozen with awe. It was a Christmas card from Nicole, mailed just a day or two before her accident. Tears filled my eyes immediately, feeling like she had granted my wish. Even though I didn't think I would ever get that desire fulfilled, I was hearing from her one last time. It was wonderful. I cherished every word she wrote, every expression of kindness, enthusiasm, and encouragement. She wished me a good time in Costa Rica, hoped the final year of my master's degree was going well, and said that she couldn't wait to attend my book signing. Nicole signed off as she always did: "Love, Babydoll." It was yet another beautiful miracle in the journey of my grief.

My grief was big, as big as my love. I believe that is the very essence of beauty in grief—that it is based in love. If we didn't love, we wouldn't grieve. Grief is the organic expression of love when loss of any kind is experienced. And when love is offered to the grief, it need not be feared, denied, repressed, or made to feel ashamed. Grief is a natural, full-being expression of love that takes its time, that has its own rhythm, pace, and texture. Grief allowed, respected, and made space for is grief endured, healed, and made beautiful.

Beauty tips for grief

1. Consider one of the deepest losses you have experienced in your life. Name it. Who did you lose? What did you lose? When was it? How old were you when you experienced this loss? Who was around you? Where were you? What did you do with your feelings of loss at that time? Try to remember all that you can, in as much detail as possible. Journal your thoughts around this and/or bring it in confidence to a loved one who you trust.

2. How have you defended against really feeling the grief associated with this loss? What has been your MO (modus operandi)? How have you created distractions to avoid feeling your grief, i.e. through drinking, drugging, sex, workaholism, compulsive/obsessive behaviors, etc.? You might know immediately what your MO has been or you may be blind to it. If the latter is the case, ask the universe to help you recognize your patterns around resisting your grief. That is the first step.

3. If you don't defend against this loss or remain frozen in anxiety over it—because the feeling is too big to feel, or because it might overwhelm and consume you—what would happen? Can you try it for one day? One week? What if you didn't eat that extra dessert, or smoke that next cigarette, or get lost in the Internet? Notice. Lovingly observe yourself, and remember that you are fully capable of containing and flowing with any emotions that come up. First step: breathe.

4. Honour your grief in a special way. For example, go to the grave of someone you lost and offer a flower in gratitude for how he or she touched your life; speak to their spirits even as you stand above the ashes of the bodies they no longer inhabit. Write a letter to the one

you lost, saying everything you wish you could say in person and trust that on some level, he or she is hearing you. And then, once you are done, write a letter back to yourself from that person. From the love in your heart, channel their spirit and take in the message offered to you. This may feel strange and unreal at first, but do your best to trust what comes. It is a very powerful and healing exercise. Allow your grief to reveal its intrinsic beauty.

Chapter 11

The Beauty Of Forgiveness

"Forgiveness offers everything (you) want ... It sparkles on your eyes as you awake, and gives you joy with which to meet the day. It soothes your forehead while you sleep, and rests upon your eyelids so you see no dreams of fear and evil, malice and attack. And when you wake again, it offers you another day of happiness and peace. All this forgiveness offers you, and more."
A Course in Miracles (Lesson 122)

"Forgiveness means letting go of needing the past to be anything other than what it was, of needing the present to be anything other than what it is, and of needing the future to be anything other than what it will be."
Anonymous

Giving forth love

Forgiveness is a highly charged topic. Many people agree wholeheartedly with the principle of it—how healing forgiveness is and how much freedom it brings—and yet they are in the dark as to how to apply it in their particular situation. When it is personal, forgiving is not so easy, especially when we believe the people who hurt us don't have the right to be forgiven, or when we fear that to forgive them means to somehow condone their hurtful behavior.

We actually fear it would be dangerous to forgive in these cases; perhaps we are afraid of what the world might become if people aren't punished for the wrongs they inflict on others.

Here is where a misconception must be clarified before moving forward. To forgive is not to say that the hurt didn't happen, that there wasn't a perpetrator and a victim, or that certain behavior isn't harmful and hard to understand. To forgive is to say that even knowing all that, knowing the hurt, the pain, and the harmfulness of whatever was said or done, we are willing to come to a new understanding and to let go of the pain that thrives in the toxic environment of bitterness and resentment. We are willing to stop draining our energies into a past hurt. We are willing to see whoever hurt us differently, perhaps viewing their hurtful behavior as a call for love. We are willing to look within ourselves to see why that person's words and behaviour hurt us so much. Even if it seems impossible, we are willing to be open to a miracle (a miracle being defined here as a shift from fear to love). We are willing to let go in the name of peace, so that we add to the beauty of love in this world rather than continuing to suffer in the ugly grip of fear. We are willing to let go. Forgiveness is a brave, beautiful, radical act of love. Whatever happens in the other person's life or mind is out of our control, but our true peace is independent of these factors.

Forgiveness is an empowered choice that at times requires a great deal of courage and effort, a moment-to-moment love-exercise; at other times, it is an experience of great grace that feels effortless. I think it is a common misconception that once something is forgiven, it is a done deal. In my personal experience, forgiveness is actually quite dynamic, more of an ongoing practice than a completed achievement. I have always loved the inspiring quote at the beginning of this chapter, the one from *A Course in Miracles* about forgiveness offering everything I want. Why does it speak so poignantly to me? Possibly because I have suffered so intensely from a lack of forgiveness—both on my part and that of others in my life—and the peace and grace that forgiveness promises is truly all that I desire. If forgiveness offers all these things and more, and I truly do believe it does, I'm in!

The relationships that mean the most to us and the ones with the most to teach us on our journey of awakening are often those in which forgiveness is called for. Elements of personal forgiveness stories have the ability to speak to us all—the need to find sameness with one another, to see each other's essential innocence, and to express humility and make our own amends for the hurts we have caused.

There is a man who has been pivotal in my life for reasons of love and forgiveness equally. In the early days, I looked up to him like a god, putting him on a pedestal no human should ever have to balance on. We had much in common—he too was a free spirit, a lover of life, an adventurer at heart. We shared a passionate curiosity about the human experience and what makes people tick. Ours was a special relationship filled with closeness and sharing. I could never have imagined it changing into anything different.

As time passed and our lives changed, I was in for a rude awakening when my image of him no longer fit with the reality I was experiencing. I began to see little by little that he was neither perfect nor superhuman. Where there had been trust, there was now a sense of betrayal. Where there had been respect and honouring, I now felt uncared for and hurt. A great many things I thought to be true were put into major question; he was such a big part of my world and now that that world had changed, I was having a hard time adjusting. I felt disillusioned, angry, and lost. If this man who I admired and loved wasn't who I thought he was, if there was another side of his life and personality that I knew nothing about, what *could* I trust? I fell from worshipping him to feeling deeply disappointed, and I was unsure as to how to relate to him anymore. The angel fell to the position of devil. All pedestals eventually crumble to dust, as they must. My image of the man I once thought of as full of goodness and beauty was tainted, and now he was held in another category of "bad" and "guilty."

In the grip of my pain, I held firmly to the belief that what needed to change in this situation was him. He needed to make right his wrongs. He needed to say, "I'm sorry." He needed to acknowledge and atone for all the hurt he caused. If he were humble enough to accomplish all these noble tasks, he could reclaim his place in my heart, I would once again deem him "good," and all would be well. To my credit, I'm a person who is willing to be humbled and corrected in the name of healing, and I believe that is probably one of my most endearing and admirable qualities. I am a very spiritual person, and I felt that God was guiding me, through his grace and greater wisdom, to discover a whole new plan for the healing of this important relationship.

The biggest clue to the need for healing in this particular scenario was our shared experience of a lack of forgiveness. With my strong opinion that he was no longer the man I loved and respected and my deep feelings of being wounded in the core of my being, I decided that, on some level, my pain must be his fault. He must be to blame for my dysfunction. Sadly, I spent a lot of time and energy exploring many possibilities that would prove his guilt and sanctify my innocence, which I hoped would make me feel okay again. And yet, with all these horrible feelings and judgments I held against him, what I received from him was not his remorse or any expression of atonement, but rather his own fear-based judgment and lack of forgiveness toward *me*. If you break down the word, "forgiveness" can mean to give forth love rather than withhold it. We were both in an entrenched, thick, seemingly impenetrable stage of withholding.

Binding in guilt, releasing in innocence

Looking back with greater awareness and compassion, I am able to see and appreciate that this man had always done his best, that he had challenges and obstacles of his own, that he was (and is) human in all his perfection and imperfection. But at the time of my deepest wounding, all the goodness and love that he represented was tarnished by how I felt he had done me wrong. In my anger and confusion, I accused him of awful things. I shut him out. I lashed out against all that seemed unfair in my universe when he was no longer the hero. And in the process, in response to feeling so much inner pain, I hurt him too. I may not have stated directly that I was being unforgiving toward him, although I am sure he could feel it. However, one day when things felt as bad as they were ever going to get between us, he boldly and coldly stated his stance of fierce and unalterable lack of forgiveness toward me. In that brutal moment, something inside of me died.

I felt like this man who had once loved me so beautifully, now hated me and might never love me again. He crucified me right there, on the spot, just as I had equally been crucifying him. Because of my deep pain, I had also hurt him in ways that were apparently irreconcilable even with all the love in the world. There was a dramatic lack of hope. My already fragile, sensitive heart broke in a whole new place and felt as if it would remain scarred for life. Where was I to go from there? Was there nothing I could do to heal this broken relationship? Maybe our love was ruined forever. From a limited perspective, he was justified in feeling hurt, and so was I. But as Marianne Williamson said on "Oprah" as she counselled two audience members deep in a conflict with no resolution in sight, "Do you want to be right or do you want peace?" I wanted peace while also being right, and it simply doesn't work that way. So little by little, I allowed life to teach me some extraordinary lessons in forgiveness.

Forgiveness school

Life has such an interesting way of teaching us the lessons we need in just the way we need them. One day while still thick in my feelings of hurt around this conflict, I came into contact with someone who also had a close relationship with the man I was struggling with, whom I will name Steve so as not to be confusing. This person had a gift of purity and innocence, always focusing on what was good and true more than anything else. We sat at the dinner table together and within a few minutes, we shared a conversation I will never forget. This precious being had a way of communicating the "guilty" man's innocence that was completely pure and incredibly powerful. One by one, he began pointing to various items of clothing he was wearing that the accused had given him, like his shirt, tie, and watch. He told me:

"Steve gave me this."

"Yes," I said. "Steve gave you that."

Then he proceeded to say, "Steve is good."

I took a deep breath while he stared at me intently, waiting for my response. I affirmed, "Yes, Steve is good."

This illuminated person knew as well as anyone that what Steve had done had caused me a tremendous amount of pain. But he still saw Steve as good instead of bad, and, in that moment, he was a major teacher of forgiveness to me. I had tears in my eyes throughout our conversation, and rightly so, because I was being challenged in my effort to hold Steve hostage to the deathly dynamic of guilt.

My second major lesson in forgiveness was a highly personal one. A big part of my harsh judgment and strong sense of being unable to forgive stemmed from my self-righteous stance that I would *never* do what he did, that I would never be part of a betrayal as he had, and that I was therefore better than him. We must be very careful in assuming that we would never do what someone else has done, even if we were in their shoes. How can we know that? How can we be so proud and arrogant? Life had a big wake-up call waiting in the wings for me. I was about to understand the cliché "never say never" in a whole new way.

I reconnected with a past boyfriend with whom I had been deeply in love with. There had been a time in my life when I thought he was "the one," my soul mate, the man I would marry and grow old with. I could even see the children we might bear when I looked into his eyes. Talking with him and feeling the love between us again triggered a beautiful reawakening inside of me that brought much excitement and hope. Here's the catch: He was now married with children. This was the perfect opportunity to be faced with being part of what I had always judged so harshly.

There was some healing needed between us based on what happened in the past and the pain of how we parted, and I honestly believed it was healthy for us to talk, share, clarify some misunderstandings, and come to forgive one another. But we weren't able to leave it at that. For a time, we explored talking on the phone, meeting for secret dates, and sharing an emotional intimacy that felt viscerally like making love without the physical act itself. Although I felt quite guilty, it felt right in some strange way that we were exploring being together again. I even wondered if he might leave his wife and family and we might begin a new life together. It seemed to be within the realm of possibility.

As time passed, it became increasingly difficult to feel the love between us and not be able to share and celebrate it openly. Either he was going to liberate himself so that we could really be together again, or we had to end this intimate connection. I began having nightmares about how I was betraying his wife, a woman I had never met and yet who was a sister to me in this life. How would I feel if I was in her position? Horrible. Betrayed. Angry. Hurt. And what about the children? What was I doing, although indirectly, to his children? I was in the midst of becoming the betrayer, and it was tearing me up inside. So in the end, I felt too scared to be able to guarantee this man that if he left his wife we would be together forever, and he didn't feel right about dishonouring his wife and family.

We chose to end our brief yet powerful affair. It was excruciatingly painful for me to lose him again, but I also realized and accepted that it was for the best. This experience humbled me into acknowledging that whatever happened in Steve's life to lead him to where he was now, whatever choices he had made and was making, I was actually in no position to judge and punish him. Ultimately, I was no different from him and no better than him. It was not that we were both "bad," but rather we were both very human and in essence, innocent. Even if during this human experience we behave in a way that can be hurtful to one another, our core self remains untainted. What a huge revelation, which led to a big sense of liberation. It was yet another step toward love and away from fear. I believe that Steve sensed this shift, and that made him feel safe to begin mending our relationship too, one baby-step at a time.

I'm sorry

The final aspect of this forgiveness-journey with Steve involved my taking responsibility for the hurt I had caused. I have been blessed to come to a greater understanding of the dynamics in life and love through my many years of intensive personal-growth work, and there was no way I could exclude this situation from what I had learned. After having weathered many internal storms of resistance, fear, and struggle, I surrendered into great compassion for Steve. My eyes and heart were opened to a real awareness and acceptance of how my reactive, resentful actions must have hurt him. I started to see beyond myself.

Before this time, I held tightly to the belief that *he* was the one who did all the hurting and that I was innocent. In a moment of great personal accountability, truly feeling sad for the things I had done that were hurtful to him and wanting to heal our relationship in a deeper way, I mustered up the courage to call him, on a mission to share something very, very important. For many years, I had been waiting for the day when he would look into my eyes and say, "I'm sorry." This reconciliatory statement would be the crowning glory of healing between us, and it would be the balm to heal the rupture in my heart that was created the day he said he would never, ever forgive me. But that day of reckoning hadn't come, and I was no longer going to sit around and passively wait for it. It was time for me to be bold and take a courageous step before it was too late. So I called Steve and told him there was something important I wanted to tell him. Without going into any great detail about the past, I offered him a sincere apology.

I told him that I was sorry I had hurt him, sorry I said and did things that were unloving. I told him that I knew he always had been the best he could be. Mostly, I was sorry, and I loved him. There was a silence on the other end of the line; I began to feel very shaky and vulnerable. I heard him swallow, perhaps holding back tears or possibly already crying. In that moment, without any need for words, I could feel that Steve was receiving and accepting my apology with a mixture of gratitude and relief. I felt love swell in my heart for him, and I felt free. Through my conscious act of accountability and apology, I was forgiving us both at the same time, and only the love remained. Such is the beauty of forgiveness. And our journey continues.

There is a good reason why Jesus included the line "Forgive us our trespasses as we forgive those who trespass against us" in the Lord's Prayer. Along with the daily bread we consume to sustain and nourish our physical body, we must feed our psychological, spiritual, and emotional bodies with the sweet manna of forgiveness. I have learned through my personal experience that as we all find our way through this crazy and beautiful life, it is impossible not to trespass against others or to be trespassed against ourselves, even if we try really hard to avoid it. I heard it said that to hold bitterness and resentment against someone is akin to poisoning ourselves slowly yet powerfully and often unconsciously. I believe that to be true; at times, I have been intoxicated, not in a good way, by my own inability to forgive.

The miracle

It is often what feels impossible in life that tops the list as most qualified for a miracle. I had a dear friend in healing arts school, Maria, and she and I were kindred spirits. Toward the end of our time in training together, Maria took a job at the same Oxygen Bar I was working at in Toronto. One day, an opportunity arrived through our work to assist at a convention. I was placed in charge of hiring people to practice seated massage for the weekend. Our bosses told us that we were more than welcome to take part and to earn some extra money, but only if we got all our regular shifts at the Oxygen Bar covered for that time. This seemed perfectly fair and generous of them. However, Maria was unable to cover one of her day shifts, and she wanted me to hire her for the convention work anyway, not feeling any responsibility toward her previous commitment.

I was in a bind. I couldn't leave the Oxygen Bar high and dry and didn't feel I could hire Maria under these conditions. So I made the decision to allow her to work the convention only if she could cover her shift, which she still couldn't do. Therefore, she missed out on the opportunity. She was livid and would not forgive me. She couldn't even look at me, as her rage was so strong and blinding. We completed our training together, but the tension between us was sickening. And we were in school for *healing*!

I didn't think we would ever come to peace with each other. I felt that I had done the right thing; that if I had to do it all over again, I would have made the same choice. And she wasn't willing to see that she had been unfair in asking me to disrespect our bosses at the Oxygen Bar to serve her needs. So, years passed. Maria moved to Mexico. I heard from friends that she came back to Toronto occasionally, but I was never invited to take part in any of their gatherings.

One day, out of the blue, as I was stepping onto the bus to head downtown, I had the inspiration to ask God for a miracle in my friendship with Maria. I felt heavy in my heart that she and I, sisters of the soul, remained in such a standstill with one another after so many years. It took merely a moment to ask for the miracle, to invite the shift from fear to love, and then I let it go and went on with my day. Later that afternoon, when I came home, there was a message on the front hall table that said "Call Maria," followed by her phone number. I was amazed! Could it be *the* Maria?! It was around Easter and I figured she was probably in town staying at her parents' house, so I called right away.

Her voice was soft when she invited me over to talk. Of course, I said yes. We spoke openly for the first time about what happened, and Maria apologized for the way she had acted, taking full responsibility for unfairly asking me to support her in something that truly wasn't right. She shared the troubles she was having in her personal life at that time, how she was feeling pressured financially and needed the extra work desperately to help get out of debt. I now understood why she acted the way she did and felt a great deal of compassion for her. We hugged, smiled, and just loved each other again. We were each other's Easter miracle, and I remain thankful. Every healed relationship brings healing to the whole world.

Forgiveness may not be easy, but it is vital. To hold another in guilt is actually to bind oneself in a limited and life-sucking prison. We must be vigilant in seeing each other's innocence if the world is to grow in love and beauty, rather than in the opposite direction. And among the most important people we ever have to forgive is ourselves. We are all riddled in our own ways by guilt and shame. Guilt says "I have done something bad and deserve to be punished," whereas shame says "I am bad and deserve to be punished." Both guilt and shame are nasty culprits, stealers of joy and peace, yet we are the masters of our own forgiveness-destiny. Our days will either be clouded by the storms of self-recrimination or shine with the bright sunlight of self-love.

What bad things have we done to deserve only half-lives, if that? How have we gone so far as to believe that, in our essence, we lack goodness? My friends, we have gotten it all wrong. This doesn't mean that we never make mistakes nor need to be accountable for those errors—on the contrary, it is vital that we acknowledge our imperfections and remain gentle with ourselves, reconciling as much as we possibly can with those we have trespassed against. But to withhold love from ourselves or anyone else steals the gifts we have to share with the greater world. Forgiveness truly does offer everything we could ever want. But don't just take my word—try it out for yourself. I can't imagine you will be at all disappointed.

Beauty tips for forgiveness

1. Forgiveness starts inside you with *you*. Make a list of grievances—all the things you hold against yourself—as if you were making a legal case and are acting as your own prosecutor. Let the list be so extensive that you can't imagine any judge in his/her right mind not pronouncing you guilty with an appropriate sentence. Then take that list and, one by one, go through your personal self-grievances and say out loud: "_____ [insert your name], I forgive you this grievance and release you from all the energy you've been carrying around it. You are forgiven. You are now free." This may feel fake or it may feel like a relief. Be aware of how it feels to forgive yourself. Do you deserve it? If so, fantastic. If not, why not? What would make you more deserving?

2. Now go through that same list, with a heartfelt commitment to accountability. As you read through each item, notice if there is anyone else (other than you) who was hurt by your words, thoughts, or actions. In your heart, ask them for forgiveness as well. And if it feels appropriate and will do no harm to contact that person and seek forgiveness, do so. In the twelve-step program of Alcoholics Anonymous, making amends is a very important part of the process of healing. Whether or not the other person ever responds to you or chooses to forgive you is out of your hands. But the act of seeking reconciliation is highly empowering and healing. Give it a shot. What do you have to lose?

3. Give yourself the gift of a forgiveness meditation. Take a few deep breaths, close your eyes, and allow your eye muscles to become warm and melt into the center of your skull. Feel the relaxation moving down from the

top of your head to the tips of your toes. Breathe softly. Now imagine you are in front of a pool of crystal blue water that is magically imbued with the healing quality of forgiveness. Everyone who enters into these warm, refreshing waters is blessed with the peace that comes from letting go. All the grievances you have ever had against yourself or any other can't help but be dissolved as total innocence is restored. Only the love remains. Allow yourself, in your own time, to step into these waters, to submerge, to become buoyant, and to relax right to the core of your being. Let the healing power of forgiveness touch you and bring you to wholeness in every cell and tissue. You deserve it. Everyone does— that is the true beauty of forgiveness.

Chapter 12

The Beauty of Peace

"Peace is every step.
The shining red sun is my heart.
Each flower smiles with me.
How green, how fresh all that grows.
How cool the wind blows.
Peace is every step.
It turns the endless path to joy."
Thich Nhat Hanh

"Nothing real can be threatened.
Nothing unreal exists.
Herein lies the peace of God."
A Course in Miracles

Degrees of inner peace

I don't recall how I came upon a pamphlet from McGill University, but on the cover were the words (or something to this effect): "Earn Your Degree in Inner Peace." I was drawn to this possibility like a moth to a radiant flame. Was there really such a thing as a Bachelor of Arts in Inner Peace? If so, I was ready to sign up immediately, no questions asked. I was lacking peace in my life. Still struggling with recurring health challenges and crazy family dynamics, I felt desperate to get back to Montreal and return to the city and school that I loved to finish the degree I started, this time with passion and purpose. The promotional flyer from McGill University that changed the course of my life was advertising their latest academic program for Religious Studies, which focused upon Eastern Religions. I was always spiritually inclined and sought to find the essence of beauty and love within all traditions, exploring what it means to be human and to relate with ourselves, with one another, and with a greater power known by many names and symbolized by many forms.

My background in fundamentalist Christianity during my teen years had jaded me somewhat. I always had a fear lurking at the base of my subconscious (and sometimes front and center in my conscious awareness) that there was only one way to salvation, and that all the people who didn't accept it, even if they had great love and devotion for God as they understood him/her, were damned for all eternity. I have never been able to digest this doctrine, especially since at the core I really did (and do) believe in a loving, forgiving, compassionate, creative God that lives in the hearts of all of us, no matter what race, color, or creed. So I enrolled in the program and felt like the entire universe echoed a big "Yes!" and came to my assistance every step of the way. Did I find what I was looking for? Did I attain inner serenity? Did I graduate with Honours in Peace? Well, I did graduate with academic honours; however, my journey to inner peace was far from complete by the time I held that BA diploma in my hands.

What did I learn about peace in those years? I learned that there are many practices and rituals designed to assist us humans in coming to greater psychological and spiritual peace. Our lives are often plagued by fear that manifests in a multitude of ways. I was introduced to various meditation and visualization techniques to calm and still the mind, and I had the pleasure of being in the company of devotees and academics of all faiths, living out their devotion through both study and practice.

I think that one of the greatest teachings I received during that time at McGill was a more keen and clear awareness of what the Buddhists call *"kilesas,"* all those nasty peace-busting culprits that threaten on a daily basis to hide the peace that is waiting to be experienced, expressed, and enjoyed. At the root, the greatest threat to peace is fear. When we are in fear, we are usually anywhere except grounded in the present moment. Our heart beats rapidly, the mind races in wild monkey mode, the nervous system is on high alert, and one's center is nowhere to be found. It is sad to realize that so many of us live in this angst-ridden state for most of our lives without questioning it or working to change it. It has become an acceptable norm, and that is why peace feels like such a far-off dream—something precious to achieve one fine day in the distant future or possibly in some faraway land. But what if we were able to cultivate and practice peace here and now and live with peace as our new norm? We can.

I believe that the treasure of peace dwelling undisturbed within us is often masked and hidden, much like the Golden Buddha. There is a story in Buddhist lore about a statue of the Awakened One that was made of clay. It seemed from the outside to be worth not much at all, composed of base materials. However, one day a young man accidentally created a chip in the statue and, to his surprise, found a glowing golden sheen underneath. He began chipping away more and more and found that this was not just any clay statue; this was a precious Buddha made of pure gold. We all contain peace within us like that golden essence, but we need to chip away at the rough edges of fear and thick layers of illusion that keep us from experiencing and enjoying the richness of it.

Peace-busters

The *kilesas,* also called "root poisons" and "disturbing emotions," are layers of mental suffering that rob us of our inner peace in every aspect of our being. It is only through overcoming these peace-busting obstacles on a daily basis that we have any chance at true serenity, or as the Buddhists call it, the blissful state of *"Samadhi."* The first *kilesa,* or peace-buster, is greed. Greed is the absolute opposite of gratitude and generosity. Greed says, "I want this and I don't care how I get it or who I hurt in the process." Greed has us thinking only of ourselves, forgetting that we are interconnected and that the good of one is the good of all, that abundance is the law of life, and that giving and receiving are mutual partners. Greed seeks only to receive, and to receive more and more and more without ever being satiated. When we are stuck in the muck of greed, we fear there is not enough, believe that we are in need of a particular object, person, or situation for our happiness, and will go to any lengths to make sure we get it/them.

There is no peace in greed because it is a state of being forever dissatisfied—wanting more and judging what we have as "not enough" or "not good enough." When overcome by my fears, I feel like there is not enough to go around so I had better take care of myself, make sure that I have what I need, and let everyone else worry about themselves. This state of being keeps me closed, narrow, and shut down inside, and prevents the flow of life from fully blessing me.

One night early in our dating life, my husband and I were at the beach enjoying a lovely fresh fish dinner when he casually and impulsively reached over to take some of what was on my plate. My good mood was shaken as I reacted immediately with fear, threatened that now there wouldn't be enough for me, and upset with him for taking some of what was mine without permission. I quickly felt guilty for my intense reaction to what for him was a completely natural and harmless gesture. There was no trust, no generosity, and definitely no peace. Where did my strong reaction come from? I am reminded of the wise words of one of my teachers who taught that we are not really crazy—nothing comes from nowhere. The toxic greed that overcame me that night at the beach must have come from those eating disorder years when I was starving myself and trying to gain some semblance of control over my life. In those days, my body learned that it had to store whatever it got in order to survive, and sad to say, I never really gave myself enough. That cellular memory is tough to overcome, and I continue to work on it to this day.

The more I'm aware of my greed at play, the more I'm able to reveal the false beliefs that are driving me. I take a deep breath, remember that life is a flow, and that the more I share in the goodness of life, the more there will be. It is always possible to correct our errors in perception. I don't have to be greedy to make sure my needs are met—ironically the opposite is actually the case. Greed starves the spirit and hinders the mind from any possibility of openness and freedom. I am much happier and at peace when I generously share the abundance of my life, and find that there is indeed always more than enough to go around.

The second peace-busting *kilesa* is hatred. Even thinking about hatred brings a bitter taste to the mouth and a sense of disturbance to the heart, mind, body, and spirit. Hatred is at the root of all war, and it is the result of a large perceptual error. We only hate because we have forgotten who we are. So many of us hate ourselves and others and spread this toxic negativity within and without, sometimes without even being aware of it. Where is the beauty in that? Are we seeing ourselves or each other clearly when we hate? I think not. Hatred strangles the beauty of love until there is nothing left. It drains all our energy and keeps us from living our best lives.

Why are we taught to hate each other? And why do we hate ourselves? If we are all children of God and innocent in essence, what has come over us? When we break it down, we must only hate because we feel deeply threatened. We stop the flow of love and close the floodgates of peace either because we are so unhappy with ourselves or so hurt by someone else's behavior.

I watched the movie *The Freedom Writers* and was incredibly moved by the passion of the teacher, played magnificently by Hilary Swank. She had a powerful ability to cut through the blind and poisonous hatred of the students for one another, a socially and culturally inherited hatred rooted in long-standing racial prejudice. Through teaching the story of Anne Frank and having the students read her diary and create "freedom stories" of their own, the teacher witnessed tremendous transformation in how they viewed themselves and those they had deemed the "hateful-other." When guided to see their own beauty and value as well as that of others, the students found there was no more need for enemies. Genuine love and friendship began to replace the bitter sting of hatred. We are each capable of living our freedom stories and of finding the sweet joy that erupts when we become instruments of peace in our own corners of the world. We are called to transmute the heavy, destructive energies of hatred, and we can only do that through the radical power of love.

The third and final peace-buster I will explore here is delusion, which can take on many forms, one of which is worry. When we worry, we are blind and deaf to the moment and deluded into thinking that by placing anxious energy into the future we might somehow prevent the bad things we're worrying about from happening. Insane, and yet we do it all the time. The essence of the second principle of Reiki reads as follows: "Just for today, I release worry and embrace peace." This is easy to say, and yet not always as easy to practice. What calls us to be so fretful about the future that we miss out on the goodness of the present? Many of us, in our most fundamental energy center of the root, feel a lack of trust. Somewhere, somehow, we learned that the world is not necessarily a friendly place, that it is reasonable to anticipate that bad things can happen, and that we therefore need to take full control of our life, or more specifically, our future, to prevent that.

Worry steals our vital life energy from the present and places it in an unknown place and time that we can't control anyway. It is a crazy mind game that does nothing productive and everything destructive. So why do we do it? I believe that we foolishly think that if we worry enough about what we don't want to happen, we will be able to prevent it. Often, the opposite is the case, as we focus so much on what we don't want that we end up creating it. It is a vicious cycle full of anxious suffering. And what happens to the present when we are submersed in worry? It is lost. Wasted. The future moment we are thinking we can control by worrying will one day become a new present moment in which we are worrying about something else. The delusion of worry robs and drains us until peace feels far, far away.

There is a quote from the Bible about peace that, when I read it and take it to heart, has always brought great stillness and trust to my fearful mind. It is attributed to the Apostle Paul in his letter to the church at Philippi. He says with much wisdom and authority, "Do not be anxious about anything, but in everything, through prayer and petition, with thanksgiving, make your requests known to God. And the peace of God, which transcends all understanding, will guard your heart and mind in Christ Jesus" (Philippians 4:6). This statement sums up the recipe for peace beautifully. Let God know what it is you want. Be grateful. Melt into the transcendental embrace of God, knowing that you are taken care of by a loving universe that longs for you to be at ease.

Jesus is said to be the Prince of Peace. I believe he gained that title because, on a deep level, he knew his greater identity as a child of God and placed his trust in his father even in the most potentially fearful situation of losing his life. His peace came from being grounded so fully and completely in love, truth, and an amazing ability to see beyond the illusory veil of this dimension of time and space. This was the legacy I believe he wished to leave on this earth—a faith in God and in life so radical that it overcomes any petty fears related to our human vulnerability. He lived a life of truth, characterized by the very opposite of the *kilesas*—a life of generosity, love, and trust. His inspirational example is one to be imitated in our own way and unique lives if we are to live out our days in service of beauty and peace.

My piece of peace

I realize that I have made mention of the divine through much of this exposition on the way of heart awakening, the Way of Beauty, and yet there is so much more to share. Who is God to me? I believe that each person's experience and understanding of a greater power is unique, even if there are similarities in essence. Regardless of how one defines their relationship (or lack thereof) with this power beyond and within, I believe that core relationship itself is undeniably meaningful and vital in terms of the magnitude of peace one attains in this life.

Many years ago, a loved one gave me a gift, which I still cherish. It is a painting of a woman, seen from the back, with a long flowing white gown, hair softly blowing in the gentle breeze. She is standing on a rolling green hill with a brilliant azure sky overhead. The image conveys a sense of deep serenity and inner calm. Even though you can't see the woman's face, there is an aura of poise and grace about her that comes through her body language and speaks volumes. The caption beneath the painting reads "Peace Comes from Knowing God." After many years of searching for peace both within and without, having some success and many failures, I believe that saying to be true with the entirety of my being.

Everything in this world is conditional and subject to change. What is here today can easily be gone tomorrow, and what was yesterday cannot necessarily be counted on today. If we place our peace in the hands of all that is unstable and unpredictable, it will forever be wavering, superficial, and transient. Many of us seek relationships, jobs, or toys of various sorts that we think will bring us the peace and happiness we so greatly yearn for. These are what *A Course in Miracles* calls "false idols": they are the little "g" gods that can never replace the big "G" God, nor are they meant to. They promise heaven but we end up feeling like hell when we place such high expectations on the wrong things, eventually realizing that they are empty of meaning in and of themselves, and we still lack the satisfaction we so desperately desire. The truth remains: only the love we give and receive is ultimately real; only love can bring true peace.

When I was growing up, my family went to the United Church where I became well versed in Biblical stories and the general doctrine of the Christian faith. I didn't know who God was, but I was taught to pray to an unseen force that apparently listened and responded. I remember being maybe four or five years old, sitting at the base of my bed in common prayer position, kneeling with palms together in front of my heart, and praying the sincere prayer for my mother to be made well. I think it was the first time in my life that I was without my mother at home, as she was in the hospital having her gallbladder removed. I had no idea what a gallbladder was, and all I knew was that hers was giving her a lot of pain and needed to come out—and that meant Grandma and Grandpa coming to stay and help my father care for my sister and me. I wanted my mom to come home and be well, so I gave prayer a shot. It seemed to work, because she made it home from the hospital and, little by little, she recovered and life went back to normal. But mostly in church, I got bored with the monotonous hymns that had no appealing rhythm or energy. It was rare for me to hear the minister's message, because I was down in the church basement coloring photos of Jesus and his disciples and playing games with the other kids.

Beyond such early experiences with church and religion lives the beauty of the spirit. I was always a very sensitive child and had a deep wonder of creation, life, and all that it entailed. I also felt quite connected with energy from an early age, as I would play games with my eyes, consciously relaxing the muscles and shutting them about a third of the way; as we drove along the highway, I would gaze just above tree lines or buildings and would see a haze of glowing light—almost as though there were another layer to the physical structure that I could see if I chose to. I was already seeing auras even though I had no idea what they were. All I knew was that I could play this really interesting and fun game with my vision, and it passed the time on long drives.

And then there was the spiritual connection between me and my great-grandmother, Elsie Lee. We used to have a wonderful time playing games together on the living room floor. She gave me a costume jewelry necklace to keep that had white beads interspersed with lots of little plastic fruits. It was kind of tacky, but I absolutely loved it because she gave it to me. I remember Great-Grandma Lee being a very religious woman, always quoting from the Bible and being firm in her sense of right and wrong. She was the first person I knew that died. At that time, I had no idea what that meant.

I was only seven years old at the time of her passing. I got to leave school for a few days to attend her funeral in Ottawa. I was glad not to have to go to class, but felt unsure what this little trip would be like. It didn't have the joy of other vacations, but rather a more somber atmosphere. At a hotel the night before her funeral, I was sharing a bed with my sister and our parents were in the bed next to us. We had just turned out the lights, but I wasn't yet feeling like sleeping. All of a sudden, I thought I saw an image of Grandma Lee at the base of my bed, but she didn't look solid and human anymore; she was glowing with a pure white light. There was a gentle smile on her face, and I smiled back at her.

I wasn't sure if anyone else saw her or if this was a moment just between us, but I watched silently as her light body rose from the floor to the ceiling and then disappeared. I guessed this was what the term "going to heaven" meant, and I wondered if I got to see it because she loved me so much. I didn't tell a soul about that experience, keeping it as a sweet secret between me and Grandma Lee. But the following day when we were at the funeral and they were about to lower her coffin into the dug-out earth, I screamed my head off. I was livid! How could they put her down in the ground!? She was supposed to go *up*, not down. I had seen her rise and this didn't feel right. I had to be removed from the cemetery because I was making such a fuss. It was years before I gained a hint of understanding regarding this powerful experience.

What does all of this have to do with God? Well, I suppose it started with having a sense of something greater than what we can see with our physical eyes in this life. There was something more at play, and it seemed to be neutral, loving, and good. I learned more about God as he is understood from the Christian perspective when I turned thirteen and my parents sent me to a summer camp that was famous for its sports activities as well as its strong Christian foundation. as Along with playing tennis, learning to windsurf, swim, canoe, kayak and water-ski, I attended Bible studies and listened to these beautiful, loving people talk about God and life and the need to accept Jesus into your heart if you were to be saved from eternal damnation. The love part sounded fantastic, but the fear of hell and death was downright scary.

There was a powerful focus in the camp on "becoming a Christian," of giving your life, heart, and soul to Jesus and beginning a personal relationship with Christ. I was hesitant to make this commitment, partly because I didn't want to become a "Jesus-freak" and partly because if I was to make such a big choice for my life and soul, I wanted to know more about it. It wasn't until I was sixteen and had experienced the loss of two people close to me that I made a decision that would change the course of my life. Within a year, both my father's best friend and my mother's brother died. The first, Phil, died of cancer. It was a total mystery to me how a man who lived such a clean and healthy existence could have his whole being eaten away by this horrible disease. And the second, my uncle Ron, died of alcohol poisoning when his kidneys and liver failed after many years of fighting alcoholism, unable to beat it. Both deaths seemed so unfair, harsh, and scary to me.

I remember a conversation I had with my camp counsellor about my uncle. I was very concerned about his status in the afterlife, if there was one. If he wasn't a Christian as they defined that term, and I didn't believe that he was, did that mean he would go to hell? After all those years of suffering on this earth, was he destined to suffer even more, for all eternity? The prospect of that seemed horrific, unjust, and tragically sad. My counsellor, a full believer in the fundamentalist doctrine, compassionately looked me in the eyes and affirmed that devastating possibility to be the case. I felt even worse than before.

With all the grief I was feeling from these close experiences with death, something raw and vulnerable opened up in me. I too wanted the peace, love, and joy that was said to come from a relationship with God through Jesus Christ. I didn't want to go to hell. And so, the day I got home from camp, I had an experience that I will never forget. For some reason, my parents and sister had to go out, and I was left alone in the house. I decided to take a bath and relax for a bit. I lit a candle; the light from its flame merged with the soft, late-summer sunlight coming through the bathroom window.

I relaxed into the bath and felt a soothing energy filling my entire being. In that moment of softening defenses and letting go of my rational mind, the time had come to make a choice. No more waiting. No more pondering. No further research required. As I breathed in and out and pondered the mystery and magic of life, I chose to give my heart, soul, mind, and body to the care of God. I prayed the prayer I was taught, in my own words, welcoming Jesus as the Saviour of my life. And something happened in that sacred moment. Something changed inside. I felt that I was both held in the hands of a loving and powerful God, and that I had joined a big community of faith that would keep me safe and warm. I felt the peace I longed for. It was a moment of great beauty that truly felt like salvation. I had an expanded awareness that this deep and unconditional love, this warm golden light, this cellular experience of being a beloved child of a great God, was available to *all* who opened up to it. What an incredible gift.

Over the next years, I continued to grow in my faith, and yet I was always challenged by the fundamentalist doctrine. Yes, there is sin. The term "sin" is taken from the vocabulary of archery, literally meaning "missing the mark." When we think, act, and speak from anything other than love, we miss the mark. And according to the Christian faith, Jesus' dying on the cross was a spectacular and monumental event in time and space when one individual atoned for the sins of all the world for all time, past, present, and future. So our salvation is said to come from *only one* thing—from the acceptance of Jesus as one's Lord and Saviour. But there remains a stumbling block for me. I truly do believe that God is love, that God is good, and is a power that we can know intimately, even if it is beyond our limited ability to comprehend. However, I don't understand how in heaven and on earth he could damn his children for not making that one choice if they are devoted in their hearts to God as they know and understand Him. Is this justice from a supposedly just God? Is this compassion from a supposedly compassionate God? Is this love from a supposedly loving God? I am aware of the verses in the Bible that seem irrefutable about only *one* way, and yet I am also aware of the spiritual truths that all who call on God with love shall be saved. Love is salvation. And if God is love, as I believe him to be, then salvation is available to all who open to love.

My desire here is not to disprove Christian doctrine. I have come too far in my faith and my relationship with Jesus and God and life and love to ever want to do that. But I also want to honour the spiritual journey of all people. When it comes right down to it, there is a deep stillness within our heart when we relax into love where we come into contact with a deeper truth that both permeates and transcends all we know in this world. Biblical teachings encourage us to be in the world, but not of the world. We are to remember that we are spiritual beings having a human experience in this particular lifetime, and each person's spiritual journey is to be respected.

During the years that I turned my back on Christianity because of my emotional pain and inability to find comfort in my faith, my spirit sought nourishment in the Eastern traditions. I explored goddess spirituality, Hinduism, and Buddhism and found many beautiful rituals and beliefs that gave me an even greater understanding of the vastness of the human spirit in search of God and the limitlessness of God's love for her creation. One night in particular, when I was living in Montreal, I was challenged by the pain and conflicts I was going through with my family. I felt absolutely no sense of safety or love from the people who brought me into this world.

After yet another painful conversation, I hung up the phone and vowed not to remain in my apartment one more minute in case I got yet another stressful call. I walked out into the freshness of the early evening and looked up at the big sky full of stars, still visible even with the lights of the city awake and alive. I took some deep breaths. I needed some peace badly and knew it would only come from God. There was no other way at this point—not that there ever is. I affirmed my identity as a child of the stars, a child of the earth, a child of everything in between, and most of all, a child of a very loving and compassionate God who was comforting me, that very moment, in his big, huge embrace. This is the peace in the midst of the storm that is available in every instant.

And my journey with God continues through all the days of my life and beyond. I still have many fears and worries, and at times I get angry and greedy and feel as far from God, love, or light as I could possibly be. But I always come back. God always welcomes me home. Peace is forever waiting—for me, for you, and for all. This is a beautiful thought, a beautiful reality, a beautiful gift. May the beauty of peace be with you.

Beauty tips for peace

1. On a scale of one to ten (with one meaning "little to no peace" and ten signifying "highly peaceful"), where are you right now on the Peace-Meter? Give yourself an honest ranking without judgment.

2. Regardless of what number you gave yourself, take a moment now to close your eyes, take a few deep breaths of life, and find where in your body that peace dwells. It can be anywhere—your heart, your belly, your forehead, your left foot. Breathe into that part of you so that it helps you remember that peace always lives somewhere inside and can be tapped into at any point.

3. What are the big peace-busters living in your life right now? Are you consumed by greed? Hatred? Delusion? What is stealing your peace energy? Name it and get an image of what that dynamic is doing to your sense of serenity. Is there a greater message behind that *kilesa* at work? What can you do to transmute the energy of this *kilesa* and thus cultivate greater peace? Take the first step and do it. Where are you at now on the Peace-Meter?

4. Create a special container called "The God Box." Now gather many little pieces of paper and write on each one something you are worried about. Examples: One could say "my health," another "my relationship," and yet another, "my future." Be as specific as possible. Now place each piece of paper in your God box, symbolizing how you are handing that worry or concern over to the Divine. And really let it go. Feel how the burden of worry is lifted off your back as you surrender all that drains you. Imagine your own personal angel taking those worries from you and promising to take care of it all. Now you get to relax, trust, smile, and watch how life continues to unfold in its beautiful perfection.

5. I once read that if you are not at peace and are having trouble getting there, the best thing you can do is to come to peace with not being at peace. You can always choose peace, in every single moment.

6. Take some time to explore your relationship to the greater power called by many names, including "God." What do you believe? Who/what has helped shape those beliefs in your life? Deep in your heart, what does this force, this presence mean to you? And how do you honour the Divine in your life on a daily basis? "Peace comes from knowing God." Take time to know your God.

Afterword:

A New Beginning

Divine completion

It is an amazing feeling to come to completion with this book that
has been living and growing inside me for so long—the gestation
period was far beyond that of any potential child, human, animal,
or otherwise. I can only pray this beloved creation of mine becomes
a rich, sweet blessing to a world hungry for the light of beauty—that
the stories and inspirations I have shared touch each one of you in
a very real and powerful way. Writing *Beauty's Way* has definitely
blessed and transformed me on every level of my being. As I wrote
each chapter and explored the aspect of life at hand, I had many
memories surface that I felt wanted to become part of the book. I
was duly challenged to boldly and honestly look at my relationship
to life as it showed up through that particular dynamic.

When I was writing about The Beauty of Awakening, I was
living many awakenings. As I wrote about grief, I re-lived past grief
and moved through remnants of grief that were longing for authentic
feeling and expression in the moment. And as I wrote about The
Beauty of Peace, I was internally and externally challenged to
courageously examine where I was sabotaging the peace that I know
always lives and shines inside me. I was blessed with a new sense of
hard-won peace in the process, both by practicing what I teach and

by remembering the presence of the Divine that forever holds my hand and walks with me, and holds me in his arms whenever I need to be carried.

The most beautiful way I can imagine bringing completion to this book is to allow the spirit of beauty herself to speak directly to us all, as she longs for us to open the ears of our souls so that we can hear. Her message is both personal and universal, and she always speaks with the voice for love. God has a message for each one of you and he will share it with you through me here. We are all unique instruments of love, vulnerable to the fears that can overtake us, and we are capable of both great creativity and great destruction—depending on the choices we make a thousand times a day. We always have a choice as to which energy to feed. We always have a choice as to which little critter on our shoulder we will listen to. I am committed to continue to *choose love*. Life is a beautiful adventure that way, no matter what.

Blessings to you on your Beauty Way.
Blessings to your awakening hearts.
Blessings to all, in the name of love.
Lori Myles-Carullo

Love letter

My Beloveds:

I invite you to take a deep breath of life, and know that *I Am* with you. That might be the most important thing you ever know in this life. Can you feel it? Can you accept it? Will you give yourself permission to receive my love and presence? I truly hope so. Are you still breathing deeply?

I invite each one of you to walk in beauty. I created this world for your evolution and enjoyment, as your school for growth, and as your big, beautiful playground. Too many of you have forgotten why you came here—skipping out on life school and ceasing to play. But, my children, it is not too late. It is never, ever too late—and please, for heaven's sake, don't let anyone or anything convince you otherwise. Life is forever calling you to awaken. I am calling you by name and will never stop, so long as there is breath in your lungs and that precious heart of yours is still pumping. And actually, even when those signs of life cease, I will still be calling you forth unto the awakening of love.

Love is what *I Am.* Love is what *You Are.* If this is the only thing you learn and remember in this life and you do your best to live from this truth, you will be doing fabulously well.

I know that you have fears, hurts, wounds, and pains. I have been with you through it all. My heart cries for your sufferings, and my greatest desire is to help you become free. I know that in your soul there still live many great dreams, vast hopes, and deep longings, and that is wonderful! Never believe that I require you to be perfect in this life. Know that I forever embrace your imperfections and love you through what you call "mistakes" and what I choose to call "experiences". Trust that all you encounter on this journey is there to call you wholly *into life.*

In this and every moment, I offer you the chance to say "Yes!" to your life, to say a big booming "Yes!" to the beauty longing to be created in you and through you, and to humbly and sincerely say "Yes!" to me and to the love that unites your world in ways you can only begin to imagine. Opportunities will come in both mundane and extraordinary forms, so be prepared. There is no right way to do this—there is only the doing and the being itself. And I am here to love you no matter what. There is truly nothing to fear.

And so ...

Relax. Breathe. Smile. Let your heart expand into greater and greater love.

Live the beauty. You are in very good company.

And with every breath you take, remember that you came from love, you are sustained by love, and love is what awaits you when this life transitions into something new ... something even more beautiful than beautiful.

Always remember that I believe in you. I walk with you in

perfect beauty. And when things get rough and you feel abandoned and alone, close your eyes and remember that in those moments, I am holding you tenderly in my loving arms. And when you are ready, I will softly put you back on solid ground, and we will continue walking together, hand in hand.

Nourish your awakening hearts well, and trust my guidance as I lead you on a path with many beautiful twists, turns, and deviations. The journey of the soul is rich, full, and worth everything. Create beauty. Celebrate beauty. Live beauty.

All love,
The Spirit of Beauty

The world before me is restored in beauty
The world behind me is restored in beauty
The world below me is restored in beauty
The world above me is restored in beauty
All things around me are restored in beauty
My voice is restored in beauty
It is finished in beauty
It is finished in beauty
It is finished in beauty
It is finished in beauty

Navajo prayer

Acknowledgments

My heart is full of thanks to all those who helped birth *Beauty's Way* from a vision into a reality. I thank Francesco, my dear husband, who forever encouraged me (and often pushed me in the most loving way) to take all the steps necessary to bring my gifts to the world. You are an inspiration for this book and my life in a million ways. I love you, Ciccio! You are beauty.

To my almost-born son, Valentino: I am amazed that you are coming into this world at the same time this book is being born. You are intimately connected to my purpose of sharing love and beauty, and I already treasure you with a love beyond anything I've ever known.

Thanks to Jim and Peg Liddell—angels on earth whose faith and support gave me all that I needed to bring this love-project to completion. You are vital members of my "dream team," and I love you both very much.

I offer deep gratitude to Kathy Glass for being the first to professionally edit *Beauty's Way*, and for affirming how important it was to bring this book into the world. Thanks for "getting me" and for offering the changes necessary to make my manuscript even better without losing the essence of what flowed through me. You are amazing. And many thanks to my Balboa Press editor, Diana K. Schramer, for making the final touches so that the book was as great as it could be.

Also, thanks to those who challenged me along the way—giving voice to the judgments and criticisms that only helped to make me stronger and to ensure I was being respectful to all. I pray that the message of this book may one day inspire you more than anything else.

I give thanks to family, friends, acquaintances, and strangers who, through my life, have taught me the lessons that have enriched my beauty path. Special thanks to Rilla Clark, Penny Hicks-Whiston, Frances Bean-Evans, Janet Zuccarini, Alana Walker-Carpenter, Dr. Zoltan Rona, Jeff Brown, Steve Sims, and Meredith Keith.

My heart expands in total gratitude to God for the gift of my life, for constantly sustaining me, transforming me, loving me, and inspiring me to greater heights, widths, and depths. I love you with all that I am. I am yours.

www.ingramcontent.com/pod-product-compliance
Lightning Source LLC
LaVergne TN
LVHW011350080426
835511LV00005B/226